DEVELOPING
PROFICIENCY IN HR:
7 SELF-DIRECTED ACTIVITIES FOR HR PROFESSIONALS

DEVELOPING
PROFICIENCY IN HR:
7 SELF-DIRECTED ACTIVITIES FOR HR PROFESSIONALS

DEBRA J. COHEN, PH.D.

Society for Human Resource Management | Alexandria, VA | USA
shrm.org

Society for Human Resource Management, India Office | Mumbai, India
shrmindia.org

Society for Human Resource Management | Haidian District Beijing, China
shrm.org/cn

Society for Human Resource Management, Middle East and Africa Office
Dubai, UAE | shrm.org/pages/mena.aspx

This book is published by the Society for Human Resource Management (SHRM). The interpretations, conclusions, and recommendations in this book are those of the author and do not necessarily represent those of the publisher.

The Society for Human Resource Management (SHRM) is the world's largest HR professional society, representing 285,000 members in more than 165 countries. For nearly seven decades, the Society has been the leading provider of resources serving the needs of HR professionals and advancing the practice of human resource management. SHRM has more than 575 affiliated chapters within the United States and subsidiary offices in China, India and United Arab Emirates. Visit us at shrm.org.

Interior and cover design: Katerina Cochran

Library of Congress Cataloging-in-Publication Data: (on file)

17-0381

ISBN: 978-1-58644-416-7

Contents

Acknowledgements

I would like to thank Montrese Hamilton, the SHRM Librarian and a true content strategist, with respect to sourcing material (in Appendix A) for further study in HR competencies and Joe Coombs, a senior analyst in Workplace Trends at SHRM, for his development of the two cases (in Chapter 6) included in this text.

For review and insight of the manuscript and throughout the process of writing the book, I'd like to thank Joe Jones, Ph.D., director of HR Competencies at SHRM; Christopher Anzalone, former manager of book publishing at SHRM; and Tony Lee, vice president of Editorial at SHRM, for their numerous and insightful comments and overall help with completing this book. Thank you to Joyce Thompson Heames, Ph.D., dean of the Campbell School of Business at Berry College, for her review, comments, and insights. I would like to thank Erica Banner for her support and administrative assistance in completing this book. And, of course, thank you to my son, Jacob, who is an inspiration for me to be a role model to him for hard work and accomplishment.

Section I: Setting the Stage

Introduction

This book has two broad purposes. First, it offers tools and discussion for early- or midcareer HR professionals to develop their HR competencies. Second, it offers tools and coaching tips for senior or executive HR professionals to help their HR staff learn and develop HR competencies. The dual purpose of this book makes it an excellent guide for the life of one's career in HR.

There are many paths to HR competency development. In addition, there are many reasons why a need for HR competency development exists. The HR function is critical to the success of any organization, and the more focus placed on developing others and ourselves in our profession, the stronger we become as individuals and as a profession as a whole. It has been said that "career development" is a lifelong process that takes into account work, learning, and leisure over the course of one's career.[1] The same can be said for competency development. As HR professionals, we may have more control over our HR competency development than some might think.

Competence is a person's ability or skill to perform in a job. A competency in a particular area refers to a set of behaviors that define performance in that area. The concept of competency, competence, and competencies is somewhat diffuse, and the terms are often used interchangeably. However, HR competencies have now been defined for the profession. The SHRM (Society for Human Resource Management) Competency Model, a framework of competencies important to success in the HR field that SHRM developed based on research it conducted, forms the basis for the discussion in this book and is described in detail in Appendix B.

Competency development for HR professionals means focusing on developing personal competencies to add value to what you bring to your career and to your organization. The goal of this book is to foster a belief, a habit, and an approach that embraces the notion of lifelong learning and development for one's HR competencies. Continuously learning and taking the responsibility for doing so into your own control is key to your career success. A second goal of the book is to emphasize that part of this learning will come from your own self-directed efforts that can be incorporated into your everyday lives. Attending conferences, taking seminars, and participating in workshops and all other formal activities associated with learning and development are entirely positive and beneficial steps to developing oneself—but competency development must go beyond formal training and development.

Preparing yourself for the future, even if you cannot imagine today what that future may entail tomorrow, is a great way to focus and direct personal efforts. This book will provide insight as to how to embrace your competency development journey and the competency development of others through the following:

- Thinking about the future.
- Remaining curious.
- Encouraging new learning opportunities.
- Exploring the unknown.
- Capitalizing on all opportunities to interact with others who may be able to help you.
- Embracing failure, if or when it occurs.
- Demonstrating how everyday activities can actually be competency-building activities.
- Coaching others in competency development.
- Supporting your staff in competency development.
- Guiding entry- and mid-level HR professionals in their career journey.

Audience for the Book

- *HR professionals:* particularly those in the early- to midcareer level.

- *HR leaders:* particularly those at the senior- and executive-career level who manage or coach other HR professionals.

Broadly, the audience for this book is any HR professional at any career level. The implication is that all HR professionals, regardless of level, educational attainment, industry, or career aspiration, need to be cognizant of their HR competencies and mindful of the development and maintenance of those competencies over time. In reality, some of us do an excellent job of focusing on our own development, and some of us are quite proficient in our HR competencies. Therefore, while the audience for the book is broad and includes all HR professionals, the reality is that this book is best suited for those who have thought about their development in a more traditional way and have more recently begun to focus on HR competencies fundamental to their performance and success. Your HR level or years of experience are not the key—your self-awareness and desire for continuous improvement focused on your HR competencies are the key. Additional audiences include students who are interested in learning more about the HR profession or who are considering a career in HR. Career coaches or other coaches who may be working with HR professionals may also benefit from the content of this book.

You may think that those with more experience or expertise do not need HR competency development. This is a risky assumption. Regardless of how much time you have spent in a job, career, or profession, we all have a need for continuous learning. In particular, we have a need to maintain and develop our HR proficiencies so that we are ready for and can perform well in any situation faced. The point here is recognizing that proficiency levels (expertise) can vary and that our behavior in a given situation is both observable and measurable.

In truth, HR professionals who are early- to midcareer professionals and those who are still active in maintaining a focus on their career will benefit more than someone who is at the executive level and who has already demonstrated a high level of proficiency in each of the competencies. This is not to say that senior and executive HR professionals cannot benefit from the content of this book. Thinking about competency development from a different perspective can certainly be helpful to all. More importantly, though, senior HR executives who have other HR professionals reporting to them will gain value from learning how to help their staff develop, how to be positive role models, and how to look at HR competency development as something that can be developed in both formal and informal ways. To this end, each of the seven self-directed learning activity chapters offers coaching tips for use in providing further guidance in developing your HR staff.

Scope of the Book

The focus of this book is on developing *behavioral competencies* for HR. The eight behavioral HR competencies include business acumen, communication, consultation, global and cultural effectiveness, leadership and navigation, and relationship management. This book does not include a focus on HR technical knowledge. Of course, HR technical knowledge is important, and continuous learning in HR is required to maintain one's knowledge of legislation, technology advances, compensation strategies, and the like. There will always be a need for information of this nature. In addition to a focus on the eight behavioral competencies defined in the SHRM Competency Model, there will also be a focus on seven self-directed learning activities that any HR professional, at any of four levels identified in the SHRM competency research, can use to develop his or her proficiency.

The book covers how to develop one's HR competencies. It is meant as a guideline for anyone who wants to develop his or her HR behaviors and provides a roadmap of the activities that can be used in this pursuit. For HR leaders, the book is meant as a guide for coaching, providing guidance for one-on-one or team interaction to improve knowledge of and skill in HR behavioral competencies. As coaches, HR leaders continuously analyze the performance and development of HR professionals in their span of control. Effective coaching requires a relationship between the HR leader and the HR professional to achieve growth and development. In this case, the HR leader is a collaborator rather than strictly a supervisor. In fact, an "HR competency coach" may or may not work only with direct reports.

Format of the Book

Throughout the book, you will find a number of tools and worksheets designed to help provide structure to your development activities. Use them as is, or feel free to modify to fit personal needs or preferences. These tools are to serve as a guide for how to think about how you can develop your HR competencies. You will also find examples, tables, and exploratory questions. The purpose of these tools and competency-based activities is to help you guide your own learning and to become used to the concept of self-directing your learning and customizing your approach to meet your personal and professional needs. In addition, each section has a list of supplemental resources that may be helpful. Since this book is designed to be used by HR managers and leaders who are in a position to coach or guide other HR professionals as they move forward in their careers, coaching tips are provided throughout the book.

Coaching is something that HR leaders naturally do for their team and less experienced HR professionals with whom they interact. The aim of the coaching tips, highlighted in call-out boxes throughout the text, is to focus on HR behavioral competencies with a goal to help HR professionals become centered on the need to be proactive in initiating their competency development in day-to-day interventions. Coaching of this nature can be beneficial to both the HR professional and HR leader as it will keep all behavioral competencies top of mind and will emphasize the need to be both technical and behaviorally competent in one's role.

Does It Matter If I Am HR Certified or Not?

No. HR competency development should be a lifelong process just as career development is a lifelong process. Developing your HR competencies can help you prepare for a competency-based certification such as the SHRM-CP or the SHRM-SCP; it can also help you recertify by focusing on meaningful activities. Certification is valuable to individuals and to the profession. Embracing HR competencies and competency-based certifications are important for all HR professionals.

Additional Resource Suggestions

Duhigg, Charles. *The Power of Habit: Why We Do What We Do in Life and Business.* New York: Random House, 2012.

Gold, Jeff, Rick Holden, Paul Iles, Jim Stewart, Julie Beardwell, eds. *Human Resource Development: Theory and Practice,* 2nd ed., New York: Palgrave MacMillan, 2013.

Hall, Douglas T. *Career Development in and Out of Organizations.* (2001). Thousand Oaks, CA: Sage, 2001.

Patton, Wendy, and Mary McMahon. *Career Development and Systems Theory: Connecting Theory and Practice,* 3rd ed., Rotterdam, the Netherlands: Sense

Publishers, 2014.

Strobel, Kari, James Kurtessis, Debra Cohen, and Alex Alonso. *Defining HR Success: 9 Critical Competencies for HR Professionals.* Alexandria, VA: Society for Human Resource Management, 2015.

Tulgan, Bruce. *Bridging the Soft Skills Gap: How to Teach the Missing Basics to Today's Young Talent.* San Francisco: Jossey-Bass, 2015.

Careers and HR Competencies

Darla was an HR generalist who graduated with a BBA in HR management. With two HR internships on her resume, she landed her first job in HR as a recruiter and HR assistant at a midsize engineering firm. Three years later Darla was promoted to HR manager. Now, four years after the promotion and a fair amount of growth in the engineering firm, Darla has secured a position as the assistant director of HR for a small IT firm. This role has a great deal more responsibility, and along with her excitement for the new challenge, Darla recognizes that she needs a better understanding of the competencies required as she transitions from the early part of her career to the mid level and beyond. She has her sights set on a promotion to the director of HR role when her new boss retires in four to five years. Who knows what will happen next!

What do I want to be when I grow up, I thought when I was a teenager—and again when I graduated from college—and again when I left my first job to go back to graduate school—and again when I started to look for my next position... Focusing on your career is a lifelong process that encompasses jobs, learning, change, and development. Managing your career involves thinking about where you want to go and what tools are needed to ensure that you get there and that you do well enough along the way to succeed in your aspirations. In the opening vignette, Darla has clearly been thoughtful and has operated with intent as she has approached her career—and she recognizes that a focus on HR competencies is necessary to help pave her way to success.

Where Are You in Your HR Career?

How much thought have you given your career? More importantly, where do you want to be in your HR career in the next 5 to 10 years? Have you given much thought to your career *plan*? Career planning, regardless of whether you wish to advance or change your position, should be a continuous process. This process should include thinking about your work interests and your personal interests. Everyone has ideas about what they're good at or preferences about what they want to do. A career spans a person's lifetime, regardless of whether you stay in the same job, advance, or make a series of lateral moves. Typically, however, people often think of a career as having an upward trajectory and often view themselves or others as residing at a given level at various points in their career. If you're reading this book, it is because you've thought about your career and your competencies and you're interested in planning for what you need today and in the future, or what your staff may need in the future.

Before discussing HR behavior competencies in more detail, let's consider HR career levels and provide some context about where you are, where you want to go, or how you can help others think through where they are, what options they may have, and what competency development needs exist along a career journey. Keep in mind that the following is a general discussion and categorization; some individuals may describe their career level differently with varying amounts of experience. What follows is a guide to help create context for a general discussion of careers in HR.

Entry level encompasses jobs for which little to no experience is required. Individuals in these roles are typically beginning their career journey and have had limited exposure to the field of HR. Positions at the entry level are central to the organization because a lot of transactional work is done here, and at the same time entry-level positions allow individuals to explore their interests and learn more about the organization and the field. These individuals primarily support others in the HR function and carry out tasks as assigned. Individuals who wish to advance in the HR field may spend between two and five years at this level—possibly more if aspirations are for a steady state with little desire for more responsibility.

Mid-level HR professionals are those who exercise more independent judgment and who apply their knowledge and experience to more complex assignments. Mid-level professionals may (or may not) have supervisory responsibility, and they may have typically between 3 and 15 years of experience. How many years will depend on personal preference for position advancement or responsibility. A mid-level professional supports staff in the organization and in the HR function and typically does not drive strategy. HR professionals can stay at the mid level for their entire career if they so desire. These individuals can be quite competent, enjoy managerial responsibilities, and have latitude to direct projects, initiatives, and budgets. Mid-level professionals have more exposure to leadership and have opportunities to practice leadership if so desired, particularly if their goal is to move to the senior level in their careers.

A *senior-level* HR professional is likely to have deep expertise in a particular area or be a generalist with 15 or more years of experience. In some cases, senior-level HR professionals are at the top of the HR function in their organization. People at this level are highly networked both inside and outside the organization. They have extensive experience and likely advanced education, supplemental credentials, and expertise in HR as well as in business. They most likely have experience managing others. They have problem-solving expertise as well as expertise in forming and executing strategy. They have a high degree of autonomy. This person may be the senior most HR person and report to the president or CEO, or he or she may report to another, more senior, HR executive.

Executive-level HR professionals are likely to have at least 20 to 25 years of extensive experience in HR and/or in business. They have significant influence and are the top HR person in their organization reporting to the president or CEO. They have substantial responsibility and operate at the executive level both inside and outside the HR function. That is, they are executives interfacing with other executives and have organizationwide impact. They manage budgets, have profit and loss (P&L) accountability, and are responsible for setting HR strategy. These individuals are likely to have advanced education in either HR, industrial psychology, or business.

Greg graduated with a degree in business administration. He spent three years in the Peace Corps working in Ecuador. Upon his return to the U.S., he took a job as a payroll specialist since the role aligned with some of his task assignments in the Corps. Greg was a quick study, and coupled with his bilingual talent, was promoted within a year to payroll manager in a facility in Texas. During his time as a payroll manager, Greg attended college part time and after two years completed an online master's degree in HR. Wanting to explore a variety of possibilities, Greg took a lateral move to talent acquisition manager. He looked for opportunities to broaden his experience base and volunteered for a number of special projects and initiatives. When a senior expatriate assignment in Ecuador came open, Greg thought he was a perfect candidate and applied. After the initial disappointment of not securing the assignment, Greg approached the VP of HR at his location and asked for advice. Indeed, he was told, you will be a perfect candidate for a role like this in the future. In the interim, here are some of the HR behavioral competencies that you need to develop to be prepared to succeed in such a role. The VP provided further coaching and explained that excellent technical skills and his added bilingual skills would serve him well as would his master's degree. Seasoning and experience, the VP said, would be needed for him to develop the behaviors and his proficiency in both the business and in HR.

In this vignette, Greg was thoughtful in approaching his career, but he assumed that the technical expertise that he gained along with the specific skill of being bilingual and having experience in Ecuador would give him an advantage and entry to a position that the organization sees as senior. However, the HR VP has provided excellent coaching by directing Greg to focus on the behavioral competencies he needs. He may secure such an assignment with fewer years of HR experience due to his in-country experience, but he needs seasoning and experience in HR to be successful in the role.

HR competencies have behaviors associated with them that can be described as either effective or ineffective, and these behaviors can be delineated by level. An entry-level HR professional is not expected to demonstrate executive-level behaviors or knowledge, skills, abilities, and other characteristics (KSAOs), but an executive is expected to have the proficiency of the HR professionals who are below him or her in the chain of command—whether or not the executive still demonstrates those behaviors on a daily basis. HR competency as described in the proficiency statements found in the SHRM Competency Model build on one another from level to level. Regardless of your career level, thinking about where you have been and where you want to go is important. Consideration about your career should be done in conjunction with reflection about your preparedness and your competencies with respect to each position and each career move you consider.

Why Focus on HR Competencies?

Developing competencies means that you must first know what HR competencies are essential for you and your role, and you must be *aware* that you need to focus on them and develop them. HR competency development takes place over time. It does not happen by taking a class—though this definitely contributes to your development—and it does not happen by just attending a conference—though this too can contribute to your development. Awareness is critical because it means that your need and motivation for developing your HR competencies are part of your consciousness. In fact, when you are cognizant of your HR competency needs, all the things you do, like taking seminars or attending conferences, will be even more effective in your development efforts. The need for focus is simple; we must demonstrate our competency every day. Our situations and needs are constantly evolving, and we must therefore continuously learn.

Awareness starts with understanding the eight behavioral and one technical competency that Society for Human Resource Management (SHRM) research has shown HR professionals need to demonstrate.[1] Second, you must analyze personal proficiency in each competency and understand this in the context of your current role as well as of roles you may aspire to in the future. Even if you deem yourself or others deem you highly proficient in one or more of the competencies, continued focus and awareness are still warranted. New situations, experiences, and people will always be encountered, and the more we hone our skills, the better prepared we will be to handle them. Third, in addition to thinking about areas for your own development, you need to be aware that development can occur in many ways and through personal efforts. Through your motivation and focus, you can work on your development with or without people formally knowing you are doing so and with or without a lot of fanfare. It works like an air conditioner or heating system—always on and working seamlessly in the background. Awareness of our HR competency needs is a little bit like a diet; most of us know how to diet. We may be aware that we have a few (or many) pounds to lose, and we may be aware of our problem areas (such as portion control, too much fat or sugar, or too many carbs). However, without the motivation and focus as well as the proper tools, our dieting efforts will be less effective.

Exploring and defining which competencies are necessary for your success in the HR profession at any given point in your career can help you do the following:
- Ensure that you demonstrate sufficient expertise in performing your job.

- Facilitate greater success in recruitment and selection when searching for a new position or promotion.

- Evaluate your performance more effectively.

- Identify your skill and competency gaps more efficiently and effectively.

- Provide guidance for customized training and professional development.

- Plan sufficiently for succession for yourself or for the position in which you reside.

- Facilitate change management more efficiently and effectively so others see your development and recognize your growth.

The SHRM Competency Model

The SHRM Competency Model[2] was created to address a need within the HR profession (for additional details, see Appendix B). For decades, HR professionals have been developing themselves with a variety of approaches, and over the years the theme of being a business professional, not just an HR expert, has taken hold. Over the previous decades a variety of HR competency models and approaches have been successfully launched by SHRM and others in the profession.[3] In recent times, as the business environment has become more complex, litigious, and global, it became clear that these approaches and models were no longer sufficient.

As a result, in 2011 SHRM undertook an unprecedented comprehensive study and effort to create an HR competency model that covers every level and every aspect of HR competency—not just functional HR knowledge. The result has been groundbreaking for the profession. The model has already been used and admired by tens of thousands of HR professionals across the globe. It forms the basis for the SHRM certifications (SHRM-CP and SHRM-SCP) and is an organizing principle for conference and professional development for the society. More than this, individuals, organizations, and universities have embraced the model. See the text box for some recent comments. The model is comprehensive and focuses not only on knowledge of HR but also on the behaviors an HR professional needs to display and master to be successful in HR. Figure 1.1 illustrates the SHRM Competency Model.

I think SHRM has arrived at a very good definition of what constitutes success in the HR profession.—Richard Wellins, senior vice president of Development Dimensions International

We conducted a "criterion validation" study, which showed the positive correlation between the skills identified in the SHRM competency model and organizational performance.—Bette Francis, vice president of HR, Wilmington Trust Corporation

We want competencies; they are the things that make us successful.—Sharlyn Lauby, *HR Bartender*

What is exciting is that they are competencies that can be identified early and worked on as you progress over time! The "model" from which you can identify strengths, target opportunities, and develop a growth plan is available through SHRM. If you haven't had a chance to review the SHRM Competency Model, I highly recommend you do so. SHRM has invested several years of research and plenty of resources to create a comprehensive model for the HR careerist.—Robert Mayfield, director of HR

The SHRM Competency Model was conceived to help the HR profession by providing a roadmap of what KSAOs are necessary to be successful in helping HR professionals in organizations meet all of their people issues. In HR, whether you are an independent practitioner, just beginning your career in HR, or a senior practitioner, you need to be competent. As HR executives, we also need to ensure that our staff members develop the competencies they need. One way to become competent throughout your career is by learning how to learn, by practicing that skill of continuous learning, and by developing your KSAOs. Competency development as a required element throughout your career should not be treated episodically but rather as a lifelong investment. Professional development and specifically competency development should be viewed like an insurance policy. You need to pay in regularly to ensure that the benefit is there when you need it. If you wait until you need insurance, it will take much longer for you to obtain it or benefit from it, it will cost a great deal more, and it may not result in providing you with what you need. And like dieting, the less you focus now, the more you have to focus at a later time rather than continuously being conscious of our everyday food choices.

FIGURE 1.1

As an HR professional, how do you distinguish yourself from your peers both in and outside HR, and how do you ensure that you have the competency necessary to be successful? Consider the following questions:

- How do we become competent?
- How do we know if we are competent for our current level or for the level to which we aspire?
- How do we get better at what we do?
- How do we develop our skills and abilities?
- How do we decide what we need to be able to *do* versus what we need to *know*?
- How do we know when we need to develop our skills and abilities beyond where they are?
- How do we know when an experience will be helpful in developing our competencies?
- How do we learn from an experience that may not have gone smoothly?

Questions such as these lead individuals to think about both their competencies and their careers overall. Competency development can be valuable for one's job but also relates to the bigger picture of one's career. Career planning is something that individuals think about and should pursue in a systematic way; it is not done once or just when it is time to find a new job. Instead, career planning is like a business plan for your organization or business unit in which goals and objectives are reviewed and updated on a regular basis to maintain competitiveness and ensure continued success. It needs to be a continuous process during which an individual assesses his or her interest, needs, motivations, and aspirations. The career development process can link an individual's goals with an organization's needs, or it can be somewhat independent and focus on the development of KSAOs in pursuit of one's career aspirations.

As HR professionals, regardless of the career path we choose, we must be cognizant of our ability to perform in the position we hold or which we aspire to hold. With this cognition comes the need to set and develop career goals. These goals should be both short term and long term and should consider what the best fit is for you now and in the future. Based on these goals, it is important to map out the learning, development, and leadership activities that must be pursued to meet your goals. To assist HR professionals at all stages of their careers, the comprehensive SHRM Competency Model provides a roadmap with many possible destinations within the HR career family.

Setting Goals and Preparing for Your Journey

Developing your HR competencies can and should be a serious undertaking. As a result, approaching it in an organized fashion is warranted. Table 1.1 provides an initial organizing structure that can be used to help you think more specifically about your development goals and the development actions you may need to take. This table is presented here for your awareness of what needs to be done. It will likely be more effective if you complete this table and add to it as you progress through the book. More detailed worksheets are provided in the final chapter. You may want to consider developing a competency vision statement for yourself as an overarching goal or vision of what you hope to accomplish. Then, setting specific and achievable goals will provide you with direction and can act as measures of progress. The goals you set can be short term or long term or both. If you are an entry-level professional, you may have a goal to begin developing your business acumen, and if you are an HR executive, your business acumen may already be quite honed—but you may, for example, lack specific business knowledge in a particular industry or global location into which your organization is expanding.

TABLE 1.1 SETTING YOUR COMPETENCY GOALS				
Specify the competency (here) on which you will focus these particular goals.	**Instructions:** This table is intended as a general guide to help you organize your thoughts and goals as you review the material throughout the book. There are eight tables in the appendix of the book that will provide blank spaces into which you can place your developmental goals, actions, timeframes, and resources needed. To be effective, you will need to complete status updates to keep yourself on track and moving forward.			
Development Goal	Development Actions	Timeframe	Resources Needed	Status

Why a Focus on Coaching?

Coaching, to be effective, needs to be a two-way process by which the coach intentionally tries to inspire and maximize a person's potential. This can be done informally, sometimes with agreement from all parties, or in a more formal arrangement. For this relationship to be productive, the foundation must be built on trust. One-on-one coaching is usually acknowledged as a mutually agreed-on activity. In the case of an HR leader, part of the job is to manage the performance and development of HR staff. As a result, day-to-day coaching is like one-on-one training and is the mechanism for being a change agent within an HR team. The suggestions found throughout the book will provide an opportunity for the experienced HR professional to share his or her expertise and to help guide or coach less experienced HR professionals. HR leaders are knowledgeable resources who can and should be straightforward with other HR professionals with respect to what skills they need to develop. In some cases, this may simply help HR professionals see where their development needs are.

If I'm Already Certified in HR, Do I Still Need to Develop My HR Competencies?

Absolutely! Figure 1.2 shows that competency and knowledge are developed by obtaining credentials, engaging in professional development, and participating in activities initiated by individuals for the purpose of growing one's capability. Certification is important for helping you develop your competency and knowledge and to demonstrate that you've achieved competency and knowledge, and it is part of a continuous and lifelong process. Competency development is something that every HR professional should do over the span of his or her entire career. If you have SHRM-CP or SHRM-SCP certification, for example, you have proven that you have the knowledge, skills, and abilities to set yourself apart as a top performer. Your diligence, staying on top of HR technical knowledge, and your experience with respect to each of the eight behavioral competencies forged the way for you to attain a competency-based certification credential. You've proven that you have the practical skills, abilities, and knowledge to execute your job or HR roles in a proficient way. Just as your knowledge and experience have evolved over time, so too have your job and your career. And your roles and career will continue to evolve. Your employer may expect more of you, and you may expect more of yourself. You may look for new or expanded challenges, and you may change organizations, industry, or even location. Given these possibilities, you must continue to focus on developing your behavioral (and technical) competencies.

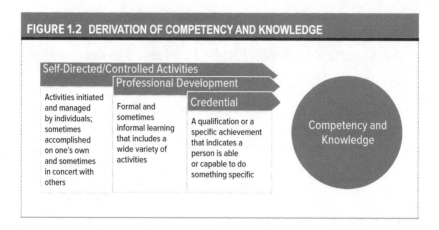

FIGURE 1.2 DERIVATION OF COMPETENCY AND KNOWLEDGE

Self-Directed/Controlled Activities

Professional Development

Credential

Activities initiated and managed by individuals; sometimes accomplished on one's own and sometimes in concert with others

Formal and sometimes informal learning that includes a wide variety of activities

A qualification or a specific achievement that indicates a person is able or capable to do something specific

Competency and Knowledge

The SHRM Competency Model is uniformly applicable to all HR professionals at all levels. However, the emphasis on one (or more) competency will increase and change as you advance in your career or as you move to other specialties or industries. So if you're already certified—congratulations on your accomplishment and congratulations for your dedication to the HR profession. Maintaining a focus on HR competencies, certification, and on your recertification will serve you well as an HR professional.

If you're not certified but planning to become certified, developing your HR competencies will help you prepare for the competency-based examination. There are a variety of things, both nationally and locally, you can do to assist yourself in preparing for the exam.[4] Classes and learning systems have been proven to be beneficial investments in a goal to pass a certification exam. In addition, since the exam is competency based, focusing on and developing your competencies will undoubtedly help you prepare for both the exam and your overall career in HR. Certification is an excellent investment in yourself and in your career. Even if you decided that the time is not right for you to concentrate on taking and passing a certification exam, learning how to develop your competencies will be advantageous to you and your career.

Assessing Behavioral Competencies

Assessing competencies is both straightforward and complex: straightforward because we know what the HR competencies are and how to define them— yet complex because assessment involves accurately evaluating one's ability to demonstrate effective behaviors. It is even more complex in that competency expectations change over time and as you move from one job to the next or one organization to the next. This is especially true when you are trying to assess your own competencies rather than that of your employees or a group of employees. Assessing competencies is straightforward in that the assessment concerns an *individual*. The target of the assessment is you, and there are a variety of mechanisms to aid in that assessment. But assessment can be complex in that it involves many components, and it is somewhat of an emotional process in that it causes someone to think and perhaps worry about what is happening or being done. To acquire a comprehensive view of your competencies, you should use a variety of methods, ranging from self-evaluation to peer feedback all the way to potentially engaging in diagnostic testing. Accurate assessment is the key to the development you need to become or sustain your position as a top HR performer.

A self-assessment is an individual's evaluation of his or her knowledge, skills, abilities, and other behaviors (KSAOs) during a specified period of time or, in this case, over the course of one's career to date. The purpose of the self-assessment is for the individual to think about and give serious consideration to the KSAOs he or she has in meeting the expectations of a professional at a given point in one's career and given advancement or development aspirations. A self-assessment is a great opportunity for individuals to honestly and objectively consider their knowledge, skills, abilities, and other behavioral competencies to document their performance and development over the course of their careers. Individuals need to be comfortable with the process of self-evaluation and must properly conduct the assessment to appropriately create a development plan or to recognize where development is needed.

A self-assessment should be a thoughtful and documented review. This chapter will help you conduct the assessment and provide you with tools and suggestions that may allow you to perform a deeper analysis and to conduct the assessment multiple times over the course of your career as you advance or as you move into different positions or to different organizations. Your assessments should evolve just as expectations of you evolve. By conducting a multifaceted assessment of your competencies and by recording your assessments you create a record for future reference. You also enable future assessments to be conducted more efficiently and effectively.

Coaching Tip

If you are an HR leader with other HR professionals reporting to you, have your entire HR staff conduct self-assessment exercises. Rather than singling out any individual who may need additional developmental attention, let your HR staff know that assessments should be done periodically and taken seriously. Once completed, you should plan to go over the assessments with each individual as a developmental activity. A self-assessment for the purpose of developing HR competencies should be independent of any performance issues an employee may be having.

When you self-assess, you become an active participant in your own development process. Your involvement enables you to honestly assess your behavioral competencies and also to identify behaviors you need to change or improve. You can then be more constructive with your own development plan as you seek to develop your HR behavioral competencies. Self-assessments can also help you increase your commitment to professional development and career planning.

Consider the notion that the questions we ask ourselves will have a tendency to focus our attention in a particular direction or, in this case, on a particular competency. Questions can also have us focus on what should be or what might be relative to our behaviors. A self-assessment is about asking ourselves questions *and* about identifying previous development experiences—and their effectiveness. Table 2.1 provides some useful questions.

TABLE 2.1 QUESTIONS TO ASSIST WITH SELF-ASSESSMENT

What have been my biggest career successes?

What are my overarching strengths?

What are some of my specific talents relative to my career to date?

What are my talents relative to where I want to take my career?

What are my biggest areas for improvement?

Where might I see my greatest opportunities?

TABLE 2.1 QUESTIONS TO ASSIST WITH SELF-ASSESSMENT

What type of learner am I?

_____

_____

_____

Am I satisfied with my career?

_____

_____

_____

Am I comfortable with my current supervisor's management style?

_____

_____

_____

Am I comfortable with self-directed learning?

_____

_____

_____

How quickly do I want to ascend to a top HR role? Do I want to ascend?

_____

_____

_____

How much time do I have to devote to development?

_____

_____

_____

Have I thought (enough) about where I want to be and what I need to do to get there? Am I a good supervisor?

_____

_____

_____

TABLE 2.1 QUESTIONS TO ASSIST WITH SELF-ASSESSMENT
Do I want managerial responsibilities?
Are there any behaviors I have relative to my career/work that I'd like to change? Or would like to develop?
Has my career moved at a pace at which I wanted it to move?

Diagnostic Tools

A variety of diagnostic tools are available today. Some are more generic with respect to personality and overall approach—such as the Myers-Briggs Type Indicator (MBTI)[1] or the DiSC assessment[2]— and others are more specific to a particular competency area. Diagnostic tools can be a good source of introspection and can spark individuals to think about their behavior in a way that may help guide them to more effective performance. In the case of the SHRM Competency Model, a set of diagnostic tools based on the research conducted was created to help both individuals and HR departments assess their performance to create development plans. Based on the SHRM Competency Model, these online tools gather feedback and create meaningful reports to help measure areas of strength and opportunity for the HR department. The SHRM Diagnostic—*Self Tool* captures responses through a user-friendly platform. The responses are distilled into a comprehensive and meaningful report that provides a quantitative baseline for development decisions. Confidentiality is protected at every turn, encouraging respondents to provide feedback to give you the data needed to better understand your HR workforce. The outcome includes:

- Combined self-reported and business case scores providing a comprehensive view of development opportunities.
- An individual report linked to targeted training for each competency.
- Benchmarks offering guidance by competency for different career levels.

Ultimately, HR professionals need to gain a balanced understanding of their HR competence. The SHRM Diagnostic empowers HR professionals to identify opportunities for development and target ongoing personal and career growth activities. Created by HR, for HR, these tools create momentum: from assessment, to development, to achievement. HR individuals assess core HR competencies, identify areas of existing strength, and uncover opportunities for development. The SHRM Diagnostic is relevant across all HR career levels, organization sizes and sectors, and is applicable in a global context—it is even translated into more than 50 languages. Benefits of this tool include:

- Balanced understanding of competencies through subjective (self-review) and objective (business case scenarios) components.
- Benchmarks that provide a quantitative comparison for your reference.
- Individual reports linked to targeted training resources.
- Competencies weighted by career level.
- Diagnostic tool created specifically for HR.

Although diagnostic tools of all types can be helpful, they are not required to begin and continue self-assessment exercises over the course of one's career.

Other Assessment Tools

A variety of assessment tools exist. In fact, validated assessment tools have proliferated the business landscape. To begin, you should first consider what assessments you've had over the course of your career. This inventory can be insightful and can also suggest where and what type of supplemental assessments you may want. To be more specific in conducting a self-assessment about your HR competencies, ask yourself a series of questions for each behavioral competency and then complete the grid in Worksheet 2.1. The broad questions to consider in completing the worksheet are:

- What assessments have I completed that will provide insight into a particular competency?
- Have I completed multiple assessments over time that will shed light on development and evolution of KSAOs for each competency?
- Can I distinguish my performance and assessment of my performance at different levels?
- Once completed, where do the gaps exist and for which competencies?

Note: It is entirely possible that one assessment will provide insight for more than one competency, so don't worry about listing the same assessment evidence for multiple competencies—but be sure that it will truly provide you with needed insights for each.

More specific questions to help you compile your assessment inventory are in Exercise 2.1.

WORKSHEET 2.1 INVENTORY OF ASSESSMENT DATA					
Behavioral Competency	**Evidence of Performance**	**Level**			
		Entry	Mid	Senior	Exec
Business Acumen					
Communication					
Consultation					
Critical Evaluation					
Ethical Practice					
Global and Cultural Effectiveness					
Leadership and Navigation					
Relationship Management					

Instructions: Read and familiarize yourself with the definitions and descriptions of the eight HR competencies presented in Exercises 2.1-2.8. Additional data can be found on the SHRM website (www.shrm.org/hrcompetencies) or from other sources. Think about where you might find assessment data as identified in Exercise 2.1. Create a more specific inventory, with breakdown, for this worksheet.

EXERCISE 2.1 WHAT SELF-ASSESSMENT OR ASSESSMENT DOCUMENTS ALREADY EXIST?

Instructions: Consider all of the assessments you've had over the course of your career from early input to more recent and more formal assessments. This may include assessments conducted prior to your HR career or outside of customary HR roles. Here are some possibilities to consider:

Performance reviews that offered specific and more detailed feedback of performance and for career development; could include both self-reviews and supervisor reviews.
Notes:

_____
_____
_____

Evaluations conducted by a school or (prospective) employer for which you have results. For example, some employers or prospective employers may have had you take an assessment as part of your development plan or as part of their recruitment process (for example, Myers–Briggs Type Indicator (MBTI) and Predictive Index (PI)).
Notes:

_____
_____
_____

Self-evaluations that you voluntarily took to learn more about yourself. These could be free assessments in books or on the Internet and could also include assessments for which you or someone else paid a fee.
Notes:

_____
_____
_____

Career assessments or self-assessments that you have pursued individually, independently of an employer or school setting.
Notes:

_____
_____
_____

Any informal assessments that you may have done; for example, did you ever sit down with a notebook and just start writing about what you do well and what areas need improvement? If you keep or kept a diary, for example, this may be an unexpected source of assessment information.
Notes:

_____
_____
_____

Coaching Tip

Look for common assessments among your staff and colleagues that they may have taken over the course of their careers to find opportunities to discuss the assessments and what they mean for individuals and the group. Having specific assessments (such as MBTI, DiSC) as common denominators can provide a meaningful jumping-off point for further discussion.

Organizing and Optimizing Your Assessment

When answering the questions in Exercise 2.1 and completing the exercise in Worksheet 2.1, you are organizing your assessment in a meaningful way. The chart and tables will help you prepare for a more detailed assessment by organizing your thoughts and identifying what sources may exist for input to your self-assessment. Your approach to these exercises should be thoughtful and follow some simple but helpful guidance. Be sure to take enough time and focus on this exercise in a relaxed and quiet environment. The more thoughtful you are, the better the outcome.

Recall Performance and Highlight the Significant Things You Can Do

Try to remember examples of your behavior from performance reviews that demonstrate strength in areas or that indicate areas for improvement. Do not assume that one positive example means that you are consistently proficient at a certain level. Similarly, don't assume that one or more critical examples mean that your performance is deficient or bad.

Be Inclusive

Consider all your roles, both current and past. Include roles outside of your current position or outside of HR and volunteer roles outside your organization.

Don't Be Too Conventional

Since this is not a formal evaluation but meant for your own use, be informative and accurate and straightforward in your descriptions. But do not be pejorative—be constructive.

Solicit Feedback from Others

As you consider your assessment, do not be afraid to ask peers, co-workers, supervisors, or subordinates. You can tell them your purpose or ask informally without identifying your intent. If you are part of an HR team, no matter how small, consider asking your colleagues or team to provide feedback to you and to each other when completing self-assessments. Soliciting or receiving feedback may be sensitive for some, so this may or may not work as a group exercise, but it should not preclude you from asking for feedback for yourself.

Be Objective

There is no need to be overly harsh or easy on yourself. The end result of a self-assessment is best when it is accurate and impartial. Your ultimate goal is to have a gap analysis that provides you with a roadmap of where to focus your behavioral competency development efforts.

Write More than One Draft

The value of the assessment is in the resulting content and in the process it took to complete the assessment. It's a good idea to reflect and revise until you feel comfortable that you've included all that will be meaningful to assist you in developing in needed areas. Worksheet 2.1 provides guidance that will help you organize your thoughts and the gap analysis you will ultimately complete.

What the Final Assessment Should Include

A clearly focused and well-formed self-assessment for HR behavioral competencies will have the following attributes.

Highlights Behaviors across HR Activities and Career Levels

The assessment does not need to be lengthy; however, it should highlight all the major behaviors that you feel are strengths and at what level they are strengths. You must also identify areas for focus and improvement. You may be a master communicator given where you are in your career or the opportunities you've had in your current and past positions, but you may still need to develop these behaviors to perform effectively at the senior or executive levels. This may be a matter of exposure rather than of capability.

States Why the Behaviors Matter to You and to Your Career

Show a cause and effect of the competency particularly in relation to your career or career aspiration. Describe how the behaviors associated with the competency have benefited you in your career or how your actions have profited an organization in bottom-line results, either by increasing revenue or decreasing expenses, for example. Your self-assessment should paint a clear picture of how instrumental your behaviors have been to your personal success and your development. And it should also provide an opportunity to state where improvements or development is needed based on how important the behavior is to you.

Emphasizes When Your Behaviors, Actions, or Conduct Have Been a Primary Factor in Your Success

If your competency in a given area was the key to some success that you or your organization enjoyed as a result of your performance, this should be highlighted. We use and rely on a number of different competencies all the time, but if one set of behaviors related to a specific competency has been an integral part of your success (your trustworthiness or ethical behavior, for example), then note this where appropriate, and you may soon see a pattern emerge. Or, for example, emphasize the fact that you are well known or heralded for your integrity and your actions as a trusted confidant of others in your organization. Highlight your promotions, job offers, or core task assignments that you have received due to behaviors that are a hallmark for you. Similarly, note behaviors that have prevented you from attaining promotions, job offers, or desired task assignments.

Acknowledges Challenges

The word "challenges" may have a negative connotation, but the purpose of a self-assessment is to be honest about what you do well and where you need to focus development attention. If you've overcome a challenge, identify how you did this to provide insights as to how you can deal with other changes or how overcoming a challenge led to the opportunity to gain other expertise. If specific challenges exist, state these as well. Challenges can be technical or personal or due to limited resources available, but you should consider all of these issues in your self-assessment because the origin of the challenge may provide insight as to how to gain the necessary experience.

Coaching Tip

A self-assessment for the purpose of developing HR competencies should be independent of any performance issues an employee may be having. If your HR staff members are to benefit, they must feel free from *evaluation* and see that the focus is on *development*. The opportunity here is to begin a continuing conversation about HR competencies rather than a typical performance evaluation or development discussion. Focusing on HR behavioral competencies will be critical for all HR professionals going forward.

Finalizing Your Assessment

As part of this self-assessment, consider each of the eight behavioral competencies in the model, and ask yourself a series of questions to help with the assessment. Exercises 2.2-2.9 provide an opportunity to do so. Worksheet 2.2 provides an opportunity to summarize this information in a digestible format. Here, you will take the knowledge gained from the exercises and be able to prioritize your approach to which competencies to develop first and which to focus on at a later time. For a sense of what this exercise and completed worksheet might look like, see the samples in Appendix D. (D.1 and D.2.)

EXERCISE 2.2 QUESTIONS TO ASK YOURSELF ABOUT *BUSINESS ACUMEN*
Instructions: Answer the following questions as part of your self-assessment process.
How important is Business Acumen in my current role?
How important is Business Acumen to the role to which I immediately aspire, and what will be some of the Business Acumen gaps that I may need to address?
How important is Business Acumen to the role to which I ultimately aspire?
Do other HR professionals in my peer group demonstrate the same Business Acumen?
How well do I understand the Business Acumen competency and the proficiency standards?
How well do most HR professionals understand Business Acumen?
How well do I think non-HR professionals in my organization understand the Business Acumen competency for HR professionals?
Am I concerned that others in my organization will evaluate this competency differently than other competencies? Is this a problem, and if so, why?
In my current role, will I have an opportunity to develop the stated proficiencies for Business Acumen? If not, how have I attempted to develop these proficiencies and to what degree have I been successful?
Optional Variation: Develop a rating scale to use for each competency so that you are consistent in your own evaluation. For example, you may use a 5-point scale on your performance where 5 is "demonstrates very well," 4 is "demonstrates," 3 is "unsure," 2 is "demonstrates very little," and 1 is "does not demonstrate at all."

EXERCISE 2.3 QUESTIONS TO ASK YOURSELF ABOUT *COMMUNICATION*

Instructions: Answer the following questions as part of your self-assessment process.

How important is Communication in my current role?

How important is Communication to the role to which I immediately aspire, and what will be some of the Communication gaps that I may need to address?

How important is Communication to the role to which I ultimately aspire?

Do other HR professionals in my peer group demonstrate the same Communication?

How well do I understand the Communication competency and the proficiency standards?

How well do most HR professionals understand Communication?

How well do I think non-HR professionals in my organization understand the Communication competency for HR professionals?

Am I concerned that others in my organization will evaluate this competency differently than other competencies? Is this a problem, and if so, why?

In my current role, will I have an opportunity to develop the stated proficiencies for Communication? If not, how have I attempted to develop these proficiencies and to what degree have I been successful?

Optional Variation: Develop a rating scale to use for each competency so that you are consistent in your own evaluation. For example, you may use a 5-point scale on your performance where 5 is "demonstrates very well," 4 is "demonstrates," 3 is "unsure," 2 is "demonstrates very little," and 1 is "does not demonstrate at all."

EXERCISE 2.4 QUESTIONS TO ASK YOURSELF ABOUT *CONSULTATION*

Instructions: Answer the following questions as part of your self-assessment process.

How important is Consultation in my current role?

How important is Consultation to the role to which I immediately aspire, and what will be some of the Consultation gaps that I may need to address?

How important is Consultation to the role to which I ultimately aspire?

Do other HR professionals in my peer group demonstrate the same Consultation?

How well do I understand the Consultation competency and the proficiency standards?

How well do most HR professionals understand Consultation?

How well do I think non-HR professionals in my organization understand the Consultation competency for HR professionals?

Am I concerned that others in my organization will evaluate this competency differently than other competencies? Is this a problem and if so, why?

In my current role, will I have an opportunity to develop the stated proficiencies for Consultation? If not, how have I attempted to develop these proficiencies and to what degree have I been successful?

Optional Variation: Develop a rating scale to use for each competency so that you are consistent in your own evaluation. For example, you may use a 5-point scale on your performance where 5 is "demonstrates very well," 4 is "demonstrates," 3 is "unsure," 2 is "demonstrates very little," and 1 is "does not demonstrate at all."

EXERCISE 2.5 QUESTIONS TO ASK YOURSELF ABOUT *CRITICAL EVALUATION*

Instructions: Answer the following questions as part of your self-assessment process.

How important is Critical Evaluation in my current role?

How important is Critical Evaluation to the role to which I immediately aspire, and what will be some of the Critical Evaluation gaps that I may need to address?

How important is Critical Evaluation to the role to which I ultimately aspire?

Do other HR professionals in my peer group demonstrate the same Critical Evaluation?

How well do I understand the Critical Evaluation competency and the proficiency standards?

How well do most HR professionals understand Critical Evaluation?

How well do I think non-HR professionals in my organization understand the Critical Evaluation competency for HR professionals?

Am I concerned that others in my organization will evaluate this competency differently than other competencies? Is this a problem and if so, why?

In my current role, will I have an opportunity to develop the stated proficiencies for Critical Evaluation? If not, how have I attempted to develop these proficiencies and to what degree have I been successful?

Optional Variation: Develop a rating scale to use for each competency so that you are consistent in your own evaluation. For example, you may use a 5-point scale on your performance where 5 is "demonstrates very well," 4 is "demonstrates," 3 is "unsure," 2 is "demonstrates very little," and 1 is "does not demonstrate at all."

EXERCISE 2.6 QUESTIONS TO ASK YOURSELF ABOUT *ETHICAL PRACTICE*

Instructions: Answer the following questions as part of your self-assessment process.

How important is Ethical Practice in my current role?

How important is Ethical Practice to the role to which I immediately aspire, and what will be some of the Ethical Practice gaps that I may need to address?

How important is Ethical Practice to the role to which I ultimately aspire?

Do other HR professionals in my peer group demonstrate the same Ethical Practice?

How well do I understand the Ethical Practice competency and the proficiency standards?

How well do most HR professionals understand Ethical Practice?

How well do I think non-HR professionals in my organization understand the Ethical Practice competency for HR professionals?

Am I concerned that others in my organization will evaluate this competency differently than other competencies? Is this a problem and if so, why?

In my current role, will I have an opportunity to develop the stated proficiencies for Ethical Practice? If not, how have I attempted to develop these proficiencies and to what degree have I been successful?

Optional Variation: Develop a rating scale to use for each competency so that you are consistent in your own evaluation. For example, you may use a 5-point scale on your performance where 5 is "demonstrates very well," 4 is "demonstrates," 3 is "unsure," 2 is "demonstrates very little," and 1 is "does not demonstrate at all."

EXERCISE 2.7 QUESTIONS TO ASK YOURSELF ABOUT *GLOBAL AND CULTURAL EFFECTIVENESS*

Instructions: Answer the following questions as part of your self-assessment process.

How important is Global and Cultural Effectiveness in my current role?

How important is Global and Cultural Effectiveness to the role to which I immediately aspire, and what will be some of the Global and Cultural Effectiveness gaps that I may need to address?

How important is Global and Cultural Effectiveness to the role to which I ultimately aspire?

Do other HR professionals in my peer group demonstrate the same Global and Cultural Effectiveness?

How well do I understand the Global and Cultural Effectiveness competency and the proficiency standards?

How well do most HR professionals understand Global and Cultural Effectiveness?

How well do I think non-HR professionals in my organization understand the Global and Cultural Effectiveness competency for HR professionals?

Am I concerned that others in my organization will evaluate this competency differently than other competencies? Is this a problem, and if so, why?

In my current role, will I have an opportunity to develop the stated proficiencies for Global and Cultural Effectiveness? If not, how have I attempted to develop these proficiencies and to what degree have I been successful?

Optional Variation: Develop a rating scale to use for each competency so that you are consistent in your own evaluation. For example, you may use a 5-point scale on your performance where 5 is "demonstrates very well," 4 is "demonstrates," 3 is "unsure," 2 is "demonstrates very little," and 1 is "does not demonstrate at all."

EXERCISE 2.8 QUESTIONS TO ASK YOURSELF ABOUT *LEADERSHIP AND NAVIGATION*

Instructions: Answer the following questions as part of your self-assessment process.

How important is Leadership and Navigation in my current role?

How important is Leadership and Navigation to the role to which I immediately aspire, and what will be some of the Leadership and Navigation gaps that I may need to address?

How important is Leadership and Navigation to the role to which I ultimately aspire?

Do other HR professionals in my peer group demonstrate the same Leadership and Navigation?

How well do I understand the Leadership and Navigation competency and the proficiency standards?

How well do most HR professionals understand Leadership and Navigation?

How well do I think non-HR professionals in my organization understand the Leadership and Navigation competency for HR professionals?

Am I concerned that others in my organization will evaluate this competency differently than other competencies? Is this a problem, and if so, why?

In my current role, will I have an opportunity to develop the stated proficiencies for Leadership and Navigation? If not, how have I attempted to develop these proficiencies and to what degree have I been successful?

Optional Variation: Develop a rating scale to use for each competency so that you are consistent in your own evaluation. For example, you may use a 5-point scale on your performance where 5 is "demonstrates very well," 4 is "demonstrates," 3 is "unsure," 2 is "demonstrates very little," and 1 is "does not demonstrate at all."

EXERCISE 2.9 QUESTIONS TO ASK YOURSELF ABOUT *RELATIONSHIP MANAGEMENT*

Instructions: Answer the following questions as part of your self-assessment process.

How important is Relationship Management in my current role?

How important is Relationship Management to the role to which I immediately aspire, and what will be some of the Relationship Management gaps that I may need to address?

How important is Relationship Management to the role to which I ultimately aspire?

Do other HR professionals in my peer group demonstrate the same Relationship Management?

How well do I understand the Relationship Management competency and the proficiency standards?

How well do most HR professionals understand Relationship Management?

How well do I think non-HR professionals in my organization understand the Relationship Management competency for HR professionals?

Am I concerned that others in my organization will evaluate this competency differently than other competencies? Is this a problem, and if so, why?

In my current role, will I have an opportunity to develop the stated proficiencies for Relationship Management? If not, how have I attempted to develop these proficiencies and to what degree have I been successful?

Optional Variation: Develop a rating scale to use for each competency so that you are consistent in your own evaluation. For example, you may use a 5-point scale on your performance where 5 is "demonstrates very well," 4 is "demonstrates," 3 is "unsure," 2 is "demonstrates very little," and 1 is "does not demonstrate at all."

WORKSHEET 2.2 COMPETENCY ASSESSMENT WORKSHEET

Competency	Importance of this competency to my current role		I am behaviorally competent at which level	Competency compared with colleagues at my level	Opportunity for development	Priority level for addressing development
	NOW High Medium Low	**FUTURE** High Medium Low	Entry Mid Senior Exec	High Medium Low	High Medium Low	High Medium Low
Business Acumen						
Communication						
Consultation						
Critical Evaluation						
Ethical Practice						
Global and Cultural						
Leadership and Navigation						
Relationship Management						

Instructions: Now that you know more about how to define and describe each competency and have identified what assessments you have completed and which exist for this analysis, it is time to take the assessment one step further and think about your proficiency, any gaps you might have, and how you want to prioritize addressing your needs.
Note: Only make 2-3 behavioral competencies a high priority for development at one time—more would be unrealistic. Priorities can change.

In completing a self-assessment, it may be helpful to compare yourself with someone whom you wish to emulate—either real or fictional. For example, if you've met or read about chief human resource officers (CHROs) or CEOs whom you admire, try asking yourself a series of questions like the following:

- What knowledge and skills do these individuals possess that I do not?
- What life or career experiences do they have that are different from mine?
- What are some of the obstacles they have had to overcome either professionally or in their personal lives that might provide insight as to how they got where they are or how they've developed?
- What challenges do they face in their current roles that I do not?
- What are some of their personal and professional strengths?
- What are the key behaviors I've noticed that they display and that I do not?
- What is their educational background?
- What career paths have they followed to get where they are in their careers?
- Who are the mentors and what positions have they held?
- What can I learn from them?
- What mistake(s) if any, have they made, and how did they correct the error(s)?

In addition, be proactive in talking to others and in reviewing the assessment materials you identified in Exercise 2.1.

Meet with your direct supervisor. If this is something you're comfortable doing, take advantage of the opportunity. Do this as a planned exercise by using the SHRM Competency Model as a guide for the discussion. Create a context of development rather than evaluation. If initiated by you, the context and tone can be set by you. This discussion can result in support for the development plan.

Meet with others. Meet with those who have been in a position to observe and assess your behavior. These could be peers or other senior managers who do not supervise you directly but with whom you interact on a regular basis. It could even include those outside the organization, such as people with whom you volunteer.

Review your previous performance feedback. This can encompass more than your current position. Again, do this with an eye toward development. Identify the competencies that your position or career aspirations may dictate in the future. It is easy to sometimes forget the details of the feedback you've received or the "golden nuggets" of suggestions that may be captured in comments on a review. Trying to capture them and looking for patterns over time could be quite valuable.

Review all other assessments. Review the documents that you identified from Worksheet 2.1 to look for relevant data and information to round out your assessment.

Putting It All Together

For some, these exercises, worksheets, and questions may feel cumbersome or not necessary. However, the purpose is to give you time and context to really think about your personal and behavioral proficiency as well as where you want to go with your HR career. Develop a *competency vision statement* for yourself. A vision statement for yourself that is specific to your HR competencies can aid in setting specific and achievable goals and can provide direction and act as a measure of your progress. Goals can be short term and long term. If you are an entry-level professional, you may have a goal to begin developing your business acumen further, and if you are an HR executive, your business acumen may already be quite honed—but you may lack specific business knowledge in a particular industry or geographic location that you need to develop to maintain your reputation as a highly competent HR executive. Worksheet 2.3 provides you with an approach to pull this together and offers a way to think about the actions you need to take, a realistic timeline, and the resources you will need. You are likely to find a new perspective or way to think about your competencies by completing some or all of the exercises and worksheets in this chapter. Worksheet 2.3 groups all the behavioral competencies into a single sheet, starting with your competency vision statement. You may find it helpful to create a separate worksheet for each behavioral competency depending upon how many goals you are focusing on at any given time.

WORKSHEET 2.3 PREPARATION FOR SETTING YOUR COMPETENCY DEVELOPMENT GOALS

Competency Vision Statement: As you read the remainder of this book, think about a vision statement for yourself with respect to each HR behavioral competency. This will also help you think about specific developmental goals that you may set for yourself for each competency.

Competency	Development Goal	Development Actions	Timeframe	Status
Business Acumen				
Communication				
Consultation				
Critical Evaluation				
Ethical Practice				
Global and Cultural Effectiveness				
Leadership and Navigation				
Relationship Management				

Instructions: Create development goals for each competency. Your development actions should include activities that are similar to the self-directed learning activities highlighted in the forthcoming chapters. There may be overlap in your activities in that one activity may help develop multiple competencies. Including a timeline is important to provide a structure and measurability to your efforts. Finally, periodically assessing the status of your goal accomplishment will help keep you on track.

CHAPTER 3

Developing Your Proficiency with Self-Initiated Activities

Now that you've completed your self-assessments, and you have a strong sense of where you need to focus your development, you can build a strategy of how to fulfill your development needs. Chapters 4-10 will discuss specific approaches to development such as role-playing, networking, case studies, purposeful discussion, purposeful observation, volunteering, and creating a portfolio.

Learning and change for adult professionals best occur through experience and reflection. Experiential activities place people directly within a concrete situation and allows them to apply what they are learning in a more effective way. As a result, HR practitioners need to become active partners in learning new concepts or in developing and strengthening new behaviors. Activities that engage individuals in actual, ongoing work can serve as a powerful mechanism for behavior change. Experience in and of itself may not be the sole mechanism for learning, but reflection on the experience can yield wisdom and insight that will be invaluable in effective development of one's knowledge, skills, abilities, and other characteristics (KSAOs).

For further discussion about adult learning and how it relates to HR competency development, see Appendix C. It provides additional context with respect to readiness to learn and how self-directed and self-initiated learning activities can be valuable in your development. There is also an exercise to help you identify your preferred learning activities so that you can better match your preferences with the developmental activities you select. This will have a positive influence on your learning.

The common denominator for the techniques and approaches recommended in this book is that they are self-directed or self-initiated with respect to learning and development. This means that the individual is taking responsibility for all aspects of learning and development. Through your own initiative, you select and manage your learning activities, and you evaluate, sometimes with the help of others, and assess your progress. Self-directed learning does not mean that learning activities are done solely by oneself, nor does it mean that all activities are decided on and executed without assistance. The final decision of who is involved is typically owned by the learner, but the choices of what is done, when, and how can certainly be done with consultation. Self-directed learners are typically motivated, tend to be persistent, are independent, are usually self-disciplined, set their goals and remain goal oriented, and develop more self-confidence over time.

Coaching Tip

As HR leader, you may want to help your HR staff members become motivated to learn on their own. One way to do this is to show support and encouragement. But beyond this general support, discussing how you have learned some of your most important lessons with respect to being an HR leader will be influential in making the point that much of what we learn, we do so through experience.

Competency-Based Activities You Can Do on the Job

While there are many formal and informal mechanisms for learning, the following chapters focus on seven self-managed activities that you can do alone or with colleagues and supporters. You may find other activities useful and can certainly add them to your arsenal of development endeavors. Many of these activities are designed for HR professionals to incorporate into their everyday activities. Others may take a little more planning and preparation work. With all of these activities, the adult learner will need to be "ready" to learn and will need to approach the activity with thought and deliberation. The following activities will be included.

Role-Play

Role-playing is a learning activity that involves changing your behavior or assuming a role for the purpose of learning or teaching something new. One or more "players" take on a role or persona and are essentially given permission to act in a way that they might not normally act.

Networking

Networking is both an art and a science. It has the overall purpose of building professional relationships. Networking, at its core, is an exchange between two people and typically involves the cultivation of long-term and productive relationships.

Case Studies

The case study method can help HR professionals develop their analytical and problem-solving skills by presenting a story or a case, real or fictitious, about people, organizations, or situations that have been faced. The chosen scenario resonates with readers, prompting discussion and analysis to take place.

Purposeful Discussion

The Socratic method is often thought of as a form of teaching or as a teaching tactic. It can be a powerful method for directing the learner toward critical thinking. And while Socrates focused on moral education, this method can be applied to learning more about oneself and how to critically evaluate KSAOs with intent as well as to developing KSAOs based on evaluation. Purposeful discussion can lead to learning and understanding which behaviors are successful in which circumstances and which may be less successful.

Purposeful Observation

Observation involves careful watching or listening. The art of observation can be formal or informal and is driven by someone's own volition. Observation involves taking note of certain facts or behaviors and recognizing patterns—

or the lack of patterns. It may involve making a mental note of something or actually taking notes.

Volunteering

To volunteer is often considered an altruistic activity in which an individual or group provides services for no financial gain—often in the community rather than in an organization. Volunteering is also well known for skill development, and is often intended to promote improvement in an individual's quality of life due to the altruistic nature of the activity. In this way, volunteering may have positive benefits for the volunteer as well as for the person or group served.

Portfolio

A portfolio is a tangible collection of items that demonstrate what you know *and* what you're able to do. A portfolio can be useful to help identify the significant things you've accomplished and, above all, where and how you've developed your competencies. More importantly, a portfolio can help identify where you have gaps and where you have strengths.

***

Section II explores each of these activities in detail. For any of these activities to be effective, however, a person must be ready to learn. In fact, this is true regardless of whether it is a self-directed activity or a more formal activity, such as a seminar, conference, or workshop. The foundation has been set to delve into competency-building activities. Now that we understand why competency development is crucial, which HR behavioral competencies are the most important,[1] how adults learn, and how to assess our own competencies, we can turn our attention to tools and activities that will help us focus our developmental efforts.

Section II: Developmental Tools for HR Competencies

Role-Play

Benefits of Role-Playing for HR Competency Development

Assuming a role in a scenario that you may face in a real-life situation can help you learn by acting out the behaviors you want to display; role-playing has these benefits:

- Allowing you to practice your behavioral competencies.
- Identifying strengths and opportunities in your behaviors and performance.
- Helping you become more proficient at thinking on your feet.
- Developing critical thinking skills in a range of experiences—some of which you may not yet have faced.
- Building confidence.
- Offering a safe environment in which you may be more apt to take risks and test out new ideas or solutions.
- Helping develop better listening skills and promotes more creative problem-solving.
- Providing insight into the behavior and patterns of others.
- Developing a better sense of anticipating reactions in yourself and others.
- Applying problem-solving techniques and problem analytics.
- Offering repetition and reinforcement of new or different behaviors.

Role-playing is a learning activity that involves changing your behavior or assuming a role for the purpose of learning or teaching something new. One or more "players" take on a role or persona and are essentially given permission to act in a way that they might not normally act. A scenario is created, giving the players an opportunity to create a story and act out various roles. In the context of developing behavioral HR competencies, an HR professional using role-plays can gain comfort, experience, knowledge, and practice in a particular area by engaging colleagues, peers, supervisors, direct reports, and even family and friends to help them build their behavioral repertoire.

A role-play can be fictional, or it can be based on real facts and existing scenarios. The point of a role-play is to place the players in a situation that they've never experienced before or in which they performed in a less-than-optimal way. It may be helpful to simply practice a scenario involving behaviors you want to strengthen. The idea is to present a scenario that is plausible for your business or current work role—and that represents a situation with which you have had little experience in your career or in which you need practice to become more competent. Potential scenarios for role-play practice occur every day and can range from the simple to the complex.

In preparation for a role-play, refer first to your self-assessment and compare it with your aspirations with respect to your job, organization, or career as a whole. Develop a role-play or series of role-play scenarios for each competency that you want to develop. Several example role-plays and activities are presented below, but remember that role-play scenarios are customizable and scalable to your needs.

Creating and executing role-plays can range from a formal and structured activity to one that is informal and impromptu. Thinking about the informal side for a moment—have you ever played back a situation or exchange in your head and thought about what you should have said or done versus what you actually said or did? Was this a learning experience for you, and did it cause or lead to behavior change the next time you encountered a similar situation? Did it prompt you to reengage with the person/scenario later that day or the next day, to rectify what concerned you about the initial exchange? Did you ever seek out a sounding board or wish you had a sounding board to listen to your evaluation or modification of the scenario? In truth, most of us probably do this. We may confine these role-plays to our internal selves, or we may include others. The point is that we do not always say and do the most effective things and that we sometimes wish we had a "do over." Role-plays, either formal or informal, can help you prepare so that you don't have to long for a chance to refine your performance. The best way to prepare is to develop your skills and your ability to react in real time to real situations. As a result, putting some thought into practice role-play scenarios can be beneficial.

Coaching Tip

HR leaders see their team members individually and collectively in action and on a regular basis. If you've ever thought "I wish Joe/Joan had done that differently" or found yourself thinking "I wish he/she had not said that," then you have a perfect opportunity to suggest a role-play to help build effective behaviors. You can be part of the role-play, or you can have your staff members role-play with one another—with you watching or not, depending on their comfort level with your involvement.

The Components of a Good Role-Playing Scenario

If well-conceived, role-plays can be an effective learning tool. Elements of an effective role-play scenario include:

- Identifying the behavioral competency that you wish to focus on for development.
- Writing out your objective in a measurable statement.
- Briefly describing the scenario and the specific roles and identifying the one you will play and why.
- Identifying any materials you may need, such as reports and equipment.
- Describing the physical and psychological environment if applicable (for example, comfortable or contentious).
- Being clear about the role you expect others to play with respect to their attitude and posture.
- Identifying how and when to stop the role-play.
- Conducting a debriefing.

Worksheet 4.1 can be used as a guide for you to develop your own role-play exercises. Table 4.1 provides an example of what a more formal or planned role-play might entail. Worksheet 4.2 provides questions and an approach for conducting an effective debriefing. Table 4.1 illustrates how you can develop the role-play without much effort in terms of identifying the parameters. However,

WORKSHEET 4.1 TEMPLATE FOR DEVELOPING ROLE-PLAYING SCENARIOS

Instructions: Use a fresh worksheet for each role-play you envision.

Behavioral competency:

Objective:

Scenario:

Materials:

Environment:

Roles:

Conducting role-play:

TABLE 4.1 EXAMPLE OF A ROLE-PLAY SCENARIO

Behavioral competency: Critical Evaluation

Objective: In the last budget review meeting, I did not effectively make my case using evidence-based data to achieve a budgetary increase for recruitment; my goal is to prepare and be able to deliver specific evidence-based data to build a business case to have our recruitment budget increased.

Scenario: A preliminary consultation to the annual budget review meeting with the chief financial officer (CFO); could include multiple players or be limited to the CFO (role).

Materials: PowerPoint deck showing recruitment data along with turnover and engagement data; breakdowns of recruiting sources and expenses associated with the data; other data as appropriate for the scenario.

Environment: CFO sitting behind a desk in his/her office; slight air of condescension on the part of the CFO.

Roles: CFO develops the budget and presents it to the executive team; as HR generalist, it is your role to discuss why you want to increase the recruiting budget. This is a subset discussion and is not about the entire HR budget. Note: whoever plays the role of CFO will need to be coached about the CFO's persona so he or she can try to mirror it to make the situation real.

Conducting role-play: The CFO's role is to push back several times by stating that he or she does not understand the data or by saying the you have not been clear or that there is no way to make a connection between engagement and recruiting sources; the discussion should continue with you playing the HR expert having to find several different approaches to your argument with the CFO. Your role-playing partner should not tell you of his or her plans so that the role-playing will be an actual simulation of how the discussion may go. Stay in character.

WORKSHEET 4.2 TEMPLATE FOR CONDUCTING AN EFFECTIVE DEBRIEFING

Instructions: Consider and discuss the following questions with your role-play partner(s).

How did the role-play feel? Was it comfortable or uncomfortable? Why?
Notes:

_____

_____

_____

In what ways did you change your behavior in the role-play from what you've done in real-life situations?
Notes:

_____

_____

_____

What did your role-play partner think you did effectively?
Notes:

_____

_____

_____

What did your role-play partner think you did ineffectively or could improve on? Be specific.
Notes:

_____

_____

_____

What would you do differently next time you are in this scenario—real or role-play?
Notes:

_____

_____

_____

What was the tone of the role-play, and how close would this mirror a situation that you might realistically face?
Notes:

_____

_____

_____

WORKSHEET 4.2 TEMPLATE FOR CONDUCTING AN EFFECTIVE DEBRIEFING

Besides the competency you identified as your objective, what other HR behavioral competencies did you display in the scenario? Which did you perform effectively, and which may need further development?

Notes:

_____

_____

_____

What was supposed to happen in this scenario? Did it—why or why not?

Notes:

_____

_____

_____

What could you have done to be better prepared for this role-play, and what do you need to do to be better prepared for meeting the challenges of this scenario in a real situation?

Notes:

_____

_____

_____

Were the objectives of your role-play clear, or do you need to write future role-play scenarios differently for them to be effective learning activities?

Notes:

_____

_____

_____

What did you learn about yourself?

Notes:

_____

_____

_____

What did you learn about the scenarios that will serve you well when you encounter this or a similar situation in the future?

Notes:

_____

_____

_____

Variation: Many of the questions above can be applied to actual interactions and can be used to analyze how you performed in a particular situation. If you have an exchange or a meeting or are faced with a situation that left you feeling uncomfortable or thinking that you wish you had done something differently, take the questions above and answer them—write your answers down, and conduct a debriefing for yourself on a real situation.

the context that is created can provide many different role-play variations and opportunities for the individual, a pair of players, or more, if applicable.

In developing an effective role-play, you should spend some time thinking of a recurring issue that is related to the competency you've selected. Find data to support the concern, such as feedback from a supervisor, coaching from a colleague, or misunderstandings in e-mails. More importantly, think of situations in which you've been uncomfortable and with which you think you can benefit from focused development. Think of upcoming opportunities in which you will want to showcase your behavior so that you are seen in a more effective light or in a way that you've not behaved previously. For example, if there is an upcoming budget meeting and you believe there will be tension around HR expenses, such as recruitment and staffing, you may want to build a role-play scenario that can help you prepare. Reviewing the budget and building a list of your arguments are good ways to be prepared, but actually engaging in a discussion with someone else playing the role of the naysayer (for example) will make the situation real and give you practice that could be invaluable in making your point and displaying effective behaviors.

Structure the role-play so that you can practice several times. You will want to and have time to reflect about how what you learned, to receive feedback, and to incorporate what you have learned into the follow-up. You will not need to practice the same scenario each time you have an important budget meeting, for example, because the role-play will help you become more comfortable demonstrating different behaviors, and by demonstrating new behaviors you will be engaging with others in your organization on a level at which they have not experienced you previously.

Role-play can be a powerful tool to help develop effective behavior in the line of action. You can hone your demeanor to be both more comfortable and more effective. Yet role-play need not be a burden to use or develop. In addition to the suggestions above, role-play can be employed almost daily as a tool to practice and build skills. For example, if your drive to work takes 20 minutes, and you expect an interaction that day that is either new to you or that you anticipate will be difficult, practice in the car. Voice the questions or arguments you expect someone to say to you individually or in a meeting. Then respond as you think you should; say what you really want to say—even if you think you might be too cautious in the moment to say it. Practice with different wording and with different inflection in your voice. In 20 minutes you can stage a role-play with yourself. Don't just do this in your head—practice out loud—your fellow commuters will think you're singing along to a song or talking hands-free in your car!

Remember to conduct a debriefing following the role-play and to ask your role-play partner to take notes on things that you did that were effective and things that were not effective. Instruct your partner to be honest in his or her feedback and to not hold back for fear of hurting your feelings; your goal is to learn from the experience. You should also conduct a debriefing with yourself—even if your role-play is during your drive to work. Afterward, think about how comfortable the exchange was for you and whether you think that you will realistically say or do the same thing "in the moment" and what the reaction will be if you do as you've practiced.

Role-play is easy to do by yourself, with one other person, or with multiple people. There are myriad opportunities—both viable and effective—for using and applying role-play to your development in a natural way. Consider the following possibilities as well as those in Table 4.2:

- An upcoming interview for a promotion.
- An upcoming meeting that gives you pause or concern.
- An impending employee relations discussion with an employee or a people manager.
- A discussion with a prospective vendor.
- A strategy discussion with peers.
- An imminent discussion with an Occupational Safety and Health Administration (OSHA) inspector.
- A pending discussion with an attorney over an Equal Employment Opportunity Commission (EEOC) complaint.
- A discussion about telecommuting one day a week.

You may be hesitant about the above scenarios, or you may be familiar with them or confident about handling them. Regardless, how the scenario will play out is really unknown. Each of these scenarios can range from the simple to the complex depending on the factors associated with each. Reflect on your day-to-day activities, and identify some potential role-play scenarios that you can practice either by yourself or with the assistance of others. Write these down, and identify the priority for them in terms of timing and magnitude or importance. Think about the allies you might engage to assist with these role-play activities. Then think about how formal or informal you want the role-play to be. Role-plays can last five minutes or even several hours. You decide what you need and the best approach for you and your situation. Additional scenario suggestions can be found in Table 4.2. You can identify a list of role-play concepts and complete the details at a later time. The point is to tailor the role-play to your needs and to your current work or developmental aspirations.

One additional way to approach role-play as a self-directed learning activity is to form an alliance with a colleague or friend. Offer to help the person with role-play scenarios in exchange for his or her help. Be sure to evaluate how this alliance plays out. You need your role-play partner to be open and honest, to have the ability to play "devil's advocate," and to be tough on you when necessary. And you need to be open to learning and developing from the scenarios that your partner creates. In thinking about potential partners for either a one-time or an ongoing alliance, consider those who are both in and outside HR. Partners from other business disciplines can potentially offer some interesting insights.

Coaching Tip

Pair each member of your HR staff to conduct role-play exercises with one another. Pairing a junior employee with someone who has more experience can be developmental for both of them—even if it appears that one is helping the other a bit more.

Role-playing, although somewhat structured as a learning tool, is more spontaneous than other learning activities in that the interaction has parameters, but the words and actions are not planned or known to the others who are playing in the scenario. As a result, it is a great and flexible learning opportunity. The participants will all practice their skills and various competencies in each role-play—even if you purposely home in on one or two specific competencies in your scenario.

To gain the most benefits of role-playing, you can increase the salience of the learning experience in the following ways. When practical, try using an actual location where the scenario is to take place or might take place in the future. For example, use the boardroom if you are role-playing a presentation to the compensation committee of your board. Always use or develop real-world scenarios that mirror what you have or will experience. If possible, consider videotaping the interaction so you can later debrief what went well and where areas for improvement may exist. If videotaping is not possible, try audiotaping

TABLE 4.2 ILLUSTRATIONS OF ROLE-PLAYING SCENARIOS

Audience: entry level and mid level	• Providing feedback to a supervisor about an initiative that a) was a success and/or b) failed (*Critical Evaluation, Communication*). • Discussing progressive discipline with a) a compliant employee and/or b) a defiant or angry employee (*Communication, Relationship Management*). • Discussing how to evaluate potential leaders for development (*Leadership and Navigation, Business Acumen*). • Demonstrating adaptability or agility when a change occurs in a project or initiative (*Consultation, Relationship Management*). • Requesting resources for the development of a training program about effective performance management (*Critical Evaluation, Ethical Practice*). • Discussing a sensitive employee relations situation while maintaining confidentiality (*Ethical Practice, Relationship Management*). • Sorting a list of tasks (with someone else) and identifying the priority with which to handle them (*Critical Evaluation, Consultation*).
Audience: senior level and executive level	• Soliciting feedback from other executives with respect to visioning and goal setting (*Business Acumen, Consultation*). • Obtaining resources for a global initiative to rotate expatriates for developmental purposes (*Global and Cultural Effectiveness, Leadership and Navigation*). • Partnering with other executives in the organization to achieve success on a new initiative (*Business Acumen, Consultation*). • Presenting a new executive succession plan to other senior leaders or to the board (*Leadership and Navigation, Communication*). • Selling the development of a new diversity and inclusion program to drive an inclusive culture (*Global and Cultural Effectiveness, Ethical Practice*). • Promoting the use of HR measurement, metrics, and evidence-based management for contributing to strategic direction and strategy (*Critical Evaluation, Business Acumen*).

so you can reflect on what you (and others) said as a way to understand your strengths and development needs.

Role-Playing for All Levels

Role-playing as a professional development activity provides a safe environment for facing scenarios for the first time or for which you need more experience. Engaging in these scenarios builds confidence and can help not only with day-to-day interactions but also with other interactions. This is true whether you are an entry- or executive-level HR professional. For example, the military has used this training method for decades with military personnel regardless of rank, up to and including generals. As discussed earlier, some of the key benefits when employing role-plays include building confidence, engaging in creative problem-solving, and developing or improving listening skills. To engage in a successful role-playing intervention, you need to think through the scenario you want to use and develop specific parameters. Here are some things to consider when developing roles-plays for different levels of experience and for use to cultivate competencies.

At the *entry level*, HR professional has likely not yet encountered many scenarios. Rather than simply picking situations that you haven't come across, think about your role, what your next role might be, or in what direction you want to focus your career when developing a priority or related set of role-plays. Actively look for role-play partners who have more experience so that you can benefit from what they know.

The same guidance for entry level applies at the *mid level* as well. However, at the mid level you may begin to see signs of competencies at which you excel or those that may need more focus. Because a mid-level HR professional has had more experience than an entry-level professional, the role-play scenario can be more complex; for example, it can involve more data, more complications, or higher expectations. Adding dimensions such as ethical components or those dealing with global and cultural effectiveness can also make the role-play more challenging.

The role-play for a *senior-level* HR professional is not only more complex but will likely involve managing behaviors and other aspects of the scenario for entry- and mid-level professionals. Senior-level role-plays involve increased analysis of data and situation-specific information. For these role-play activities, the scenario is as much about the preparation and analysis as it is about the actual behavioral exchange.

Since the *executive level* position is by definition the most senior HR professional in the function, the role-play scenario can be highly complex or unique so that it challenges the HR executive. Or, like the military, it can include a what-if scenario that prepares the executive to think outside of typical parameters. For example, preparing for a major workplace violence incident is not a typical occurrence but may present a complicated scenario, providing an excellent development opportunity.

Chapter Summary

- Role-play is an activity that you can do almost anywhere at any time.
- Role-play can and should engage others to interact with and help you transform your behaviors into advanced executive interactions.
- Role-plays are customizable to your work, organization, industry, or other factors that are important for your development.
- Role-plays are useful within and between all levels of HR.

Additional Resources for Effective Role-Plays

Buelow, J. "3 Benefits of Making Role-Play Part of Training." *Training Magazine* (2014). https://trainingmag.com/3-benefits-making-role-play-part-training.

Chaturvedi, V. "Role—Play Method: An Innovative Training Technique." 2008. http://indianmba.com/Faculty_Column/FC896/fc896.html.

Eitington, J. E. *The Winning Trainer: Winning Ways to Involve People in Learning.* Boston: Butterworth-Heinemann, 2002.

El-Shamy, S. *Role-Play Made Easy: 25 Structured Rehearsals for Managing Problem Situations and Dealing with Difficult People.* San Francisco: Pfeiffer, 2005.

Garewal, S. "Oh No. I Hate Role Play!" *Training Journal* (July 1, 2013): 40-44.

Reynolds, L. "Stage Fright." *Training Journal* (December 1, 2014): 57-59. https://www.trainingjournal.com/articles/feature/stage-fright.

Role Playing: Preparing for Difficult Conversations and Situations. MindTools. (n.d.). https://www.mindtools.com/CommSkll/RolePlaying.htm.

Silberman, M. L., Biech, E., and Auerbach, C. *Active Training: A Handbook of Techniques, Designs, Case Examples, and Tips.* Hoboken, NJ: Wiley, 2015.

U.S. Dept. of State, Bureau of Human Resources, Office of Civil Service Personnel Management. *Planning Individual Development Activities: Tools, Ideas, and Suggestions.* 2006. http://www.state.gov/documents/organization/107870.pdf.

Networking

Benefits of Networking for HR Competency Development

Networking is always important to business professionals and with respect to HR competency development there are additional and useful benefits:

- Peer-to-peer learning.
- Expanding the circle you can count on for information sharing, advice, and referrals.
- A mechanism to testing and building your management/executive presence.
- Relationship-building skills development.
- Enhancing business acumen.
- Developing career and professional skills.
- Exposing oneself to different perspectives, people, and organizations.
- Exchanging information.
- Developing professional contacts.

Networking can be a beneficial tool for developing one's behavioral competencies. Some professionals erroneously think that networking is something you do primarily when you're looking for a job or when you want to expand your circle of business colleagues. While both of these are true, a sometimes hidden benefit of networking is the impact on understanding and developing your HR competencies. Through networking, whether or not you connect with a specific person or add to your span of contacts, you can often learn a lot about what you know and don't know and how people behave in certain scenarios. You may also gain valuable insights into how people view you and react to you as a professional.

And while it is certainly important to network with other HR professionals from all sizes and types of organizations in a variety of industries, it's also important to network with professionals outside of HR. Expanding the types of situations and people with whom you interact can allow you to think differently about things, give you new perspectives, and expose you to people, vocabulary, and ideas that may not be readily available in your existing circle. Keep in mind that networking is a reciprocal activity and that your ultimate objective is to build a relationship with someone. The relationship could last for a short time, or it could develop into a long-term, mutually beneficial connection.

Networking is both an art and a science. It has the overall purpose of building professional relationships. But what if you thought about networking as a way to build your professional competence and not just as adding to your contact list? The following are some tips for thinking about where you network and what you can do once you get there:

- Attend networking events regularly regardless of whether you are looking for a new position or have a specific need in mind. Make it part of your regular routine. As you advance in your career, change the networking events or venues to fit your time and your position.

- Volunteer to work a networking event. Help check people in, be the person who makes program announcements, hand out drink tickets, etc.

- Stay late or arrive early for any networking event at which you volunteer or attend.

- Attend a variety of networking events—select some that are outside your traditional sphere of attendance. For example, go to a Chamber of Commerce meeting in addition to one related to HR.

- Ask friends, colleagues, and those you admire where they network to get new ideas.

- Make an agreement with a colleague in a different organization (or department if your organization is large) to meet for lunch and for that person to bring someone you don't know and who may be good for you to know. Do the same for him or her.

- Set a goal to speak to a specific number of people or to make at least one connection with whom you will follow up when you attend a networking event, conference, or seminar.

- Set a goal to pitch a specific idea a certain number of times or to pitch at least two different ideas at an event or professional exchange.

- Be observant, not just interactive, at professional events. Watch how people behave, and think about what is effective and what is not. Listen to how others phrase ideas or approach topics.

- Invite someone you don't know or know well to meet for coffee or lunch. Explain that there is no agenda—just a desire to network and know the person better.

- Make it a point to meet several people at a single event. Even if you make a solid connection with one individual, try to circulate and meet others.

- Feel free to attend an event with a colleague or a friend, or to meet the person there, but do not confine your interactions to one person or one group of people.

- Make it a point to reconnect with people if you haven't been to a particular event for a while and talk about what you've been doing and ask what they've been doing.

Networking allows you to develop stronger interpersonal skills that can serve you well both inside and outside your organization. There are many hidden possibilities in expanding your networking activities. Networking may be seen as a chore, or worse by some, and downright fun by others. The greater your comfort with networking, the more benefit and success you are likely to derive. Like your golf swing or tennis serve, the more you practice, the easier and more effective it will be for you to engage.

Coaching Tip

Suggest to your HR staff members that, when they attend events outside of the organization, they focus not only on expanding their network but also on a specific competency or set of relevant competencies. For example, suggest that for the next several months any networking opportunity will focus on critical evaluation. That is, listen for and ask about aspects of critical evaluation. Have your staff members keep notes about how others in their network demonstrate aspects of critical evaluation. In follow-up discussions, ask them what they have learned about the critical evaluation competency and how this experience can benefit them.

Keep in mind that networking is one of the most effective career and professional development tools that you carry with you at all times and over the course of your career. Networking at the core is about giving and receiving information, advice, and, potentially, references or referrals. It takes time to form a comfortable relationship with another person for the purpose of asking for a referral, for more detailed information, or for advice—but if your goal for networking is to learn about a particular industry, geographic location, or other information, you may be able to accomplish this in a relatively short time frame—because you are talking to someone who is knowledgeable. Thus, in a mutually beneficial way, you are building a long-term relationship and learning valuable information in the short term.

In networking, you are looking for appropriate connections. The good news is that you control what you consider to be appropriate. To do this, you need to think about your goals for networking. You can have different goals for different events or smaller goals that feed into an overarching objective. But networking can be random as well as deliberate. You can and should plan for specific opportunities to network, but you should also be prepared for unplanned or fortuitous opportunities. On an airplane or a train or while with friends, you may find yourself sitting next to someone who turns out to be a great person with whom to build a networking relationship. In situations like this you have the opportunity to connect with people outside of your typical circles—perhaps even more so than in some of your deliberate networking activities. Networking needs to be a continuous process. People in your network may enter and leave, and many will be in different stages of development or maturity in terms of the relationship.

As a result, networking will take effort and at times more focus. But like any tool you carry with you, like your cellphone, it will become indispensable. From the delivery perspective, you must be intentional with your actions and purposeful in your approach. Start by making a list of all the potential events that you are interested in attending, or more importantly, that you think will provide you with good networking opportunities. Create a priority list of events from among your larger list. Using Worksheet 5.1, evaluate more systematically what the opportunity is and whether it's worth your time and energy to invest. Duplicate the worksheet to accommodate multiple network events over time.

WORKSHEET 5.1 NETWORKING VIABILITY AND EVENT EVALUATION

Instructions: Assess your networking opportunities and be strategic about what you want to accomplish and which events you should attend. Approach networking with a purpose.

Event
Notes:
_____
_____
_____

Description
Notes:
_____
_____
_____

Objective in attending—what you hope to gain
Notes:
_____
_____
_____

Audience/participants—how many people will be there, and what backgrounds will they have?
Notes:
_____
_____
_____

Goals—specific outcome desired
Notes:
_____
_____
_____

Recurring event or one-time event?
Notes:
_____
_____
_____

How will this event be a stretch for you? Or how can you make it a stretch for you?
Notes:
_____
_____
_____

WORKSHEET 5.1 NETWORKING VIABILITY AND EVENT EVALUATION

Do you have a connection to this event/group?
Notes:

_____

_____

_____

Is there a particular competency or competencies you hope to develop at this event?
Notes:

_____

_____

_____

What's your comfort level in attending the event?
Notes:

_____

_____

_____

Note: If the answer to the last question is that your comfort is high and that this will not be a stretch—then ask yourself how beneficial the event will be versus enjoyable. It's OK to go to events that are easy and enjoyable if your objective is to maintain your networks or reconnect, but you might want to ensure you have a mix of easy and more challenging interactions.

This is a good exercise to complete—even if you have events that you regularly attend. Upon further analysis you may find that some of your routine events are fine and even interesting but that they are not doing a good job of helping you *build* your network or your competencies. Since your time for deliberate networking may be limited, you may need to consider dropping or minimizing events that do not further your networking goals. You may need to substitute or replace these events with ones where you can stretch yourself to test your ideas in a whole new relationship-building experience. This is not to imply that you should totally drop enjoyable events, but it does suggest that if your goal is to improve something like your communication skills or executive presence, you may need to get out of your comfort zone. You don't have to be naturally extroverted, but you do need to be willing to challenge yourself.

As you approach and do more networking, don't just absorb—be prepared to share and push out your agenda. See how an idea sounds. Develop a pitch. Give an elevator speech. Observe how people react, and listen to the questions they ask you. Modify your elevator speech pitch or idea until you're comfortable with it. Be ready to tell your story quickly and succinctly. And be ready with not just the story of who you are, where you are, and what you do—be ready to test and pitch your ideas, concepts, and things in your day-to-day activities. Relationship development really occurs face-to-face. You can certainly do some of this over the phone or via electronic communications, but deeper relationship connections occur face-to-face. Interactions can be both positive and challenging. Be observant with respect to how an interaction evolves and whether you feel good about the interaction or are left feeling upset or confused.

You may be met with resistance in your quest to network. If this happens, embrace it and learn from the experience. Try to break through to the individual or learn why the resistance is there. You will build your skills in dealing with a negative situation, and you might gain insight about yourself from someone who sees you in a way you had not anticipated. It is far more likely that your interactions will be positive or neutral—and you can learn from those scenarios as well. Try to understand and think about what you did or did not do. Since networking is reciprocal, you must be open to learning why someone is not open to forming a relationship with you. Networking should not be about titles or position, but if that is the case for the other person, developing a relationship with that individual may not be mutually beneficial or effective for you. Your time is valuable—use it for something that will help you and not be frustrating.

Traditional reasons and approaches to networking will always be present and important in a professional career. But adding a focus to this activity of honing your HR behavioral competencies can enhance the experience and add value to your professional career. Network with the intent to develop your HR competencies, not just to expand your circle. Use networking to test your own behavioral competencies and to learn about others' behavioral competencies for HR. This will double the value you derive from networking. Table 5.1 provides some suggestions of ice breakers or conversation starters for networking events. One goal may be to find out about other networking opportunities, so you may want to engage the other participants in an effort to find out where they do their networking and how developmental they find the event.

TABLE 5.1 QUESTIONS TO ASK AT A NETWORKING EVENT

Guidance: Questions to ask others at a networking event to break the ice and further the conversation with a focus on behavioral competencies.

The content for this meeting has been great—have you ever come across this information before?

Notes:

_____
_____
_____

This is my first meeting. How similar or different has this meeting been compared with others you've attended?

Notes:

_____
_____
_____

Are there other networking events that you like to attend? [If there is a speaker] Have you seen this speaker before? What's your take on his or her content?

Notes:

_____
_____
_____

The talk was relevant to the topic of _____ [fill in one of the eight behavioral competencies]—would you agree? I'm really interested in this topic; do you know of any other events or materials you can suggest?

Notes:

_____
_____
_____

That was an interesting presentation. I can see some clear application for this material. How about you—will this resonate in your business? How did you hear about this event?

Notes:

_____
_____
_____

If reconnecting: Good to see you again, Dan. How do you like this group? Have you participated before? Why do you like this event or this group?

Notes:

_____
_____
_____

TABLE 5.1 QUESTIONS TO ASK AT A NETWORKING EVENT

One of the most important behavioral competencies for HR is _____ [fill in one of the eight behavioral competencies]. How have you developed the competency or seen others develop it?

Notes:

_____

_____

_____

What are some of your own questions? What questions might you add or change based on the career level at which you are now or to which you aspire?

Notes:

_____

_____

_____

Networking by Level

Networking is valuable at any level. Some of the contacts you meet early in your career can stay with you and even become friends over the course of your career. You have the opportunity to help others and be helped yourself; helping and being helped, while seemingly opposite activities, are both beneficial to developing your competencies. At the *entry level,* your objective is typically broader in terms of expanding your network and exploring new possibilities. At this stage you have much to learn and to gain from networking. You can select a wide range of networking events and may find all of them beneficial, albeit some more daunting than others. Meeting people at your level and at the levels above you are both worthwhile objectives. And exposure to all HR behavioral competencies will serve you well.

Much of this is still true at the *mid-career* level, but here you may be starting to focus on specific HR functional areas or industry orientations to build relevant networks. At this point, you will also have a better idea as to which HR competencies you need to spend more time developing. Your networking goals will start to narrow, and your objectives will be more specific. It is still a good idea to focus on your networking and be more deliberate in your approach.

At the *senior* level, you are likely to have less time to network and may already have a significant network from which to draw. At this stage you can shift more to building your network with one-on-one activities (such as lunch or coffee) than on attending larger events. Both approaches are advantageous, but due to your level and your expertise, you have more options available to you. In addition, you may have more specific needs or goals with respect to your networking activities. Given that your time is likely limited, you may want to be far more particular about the nature of events you attend or the people you try to meet. You may, for example, want to identify specific people and target them for interaction. You can cold-call/e-mail them and ask to meet for coffee or lunch, or you can seek the help of someone you may have in common with them. Don't be shy about this—networking is a great behavioral competency to have in your arsenal, and you will find that many people are open to this interaction.

At the *executive level,* your goals for networking are likely to be focused on people who are more like yourself who faced similar challenges and problems professionally. In addition, you may be looking to "give back" more to the community and business in general and to find ways to meet others who may benefit from your expertise rather than others who can assist you. The activities in which you engage may shift again from the narrower to the broader—but the context will be different depending on your typical circles.

Chapter Summary

- Networking is a reciprocal activity involving both receiving and giving expertise.
- Networking can be done purposefully by attending an event and can be built into your everyday interactions without attending a specific event.
- You can set goals for yourself about how you will expand your network and which competencies you want to target in given scenarios.
- Networking is a tool that you carry with you at all times and that you can sharpen over time.
- Networking is a way to challenge and develop yourself continuously throughout your career.

Additional Resources for Effective Networking

Briggs, H. "Engaging with Your Contacts." *Training Journal.* April 2013, 17-21.
Cross, R., & Thomas, R. "A Smarter Way to Network." *Harvard Business Review* 89, no. 7/8 (2011): 149-153.
Crowley, B. 3 Steps for Building a Professional Learning Network. *Education Week Teacher.* December 31, 2014. http://www.edweek.org/tm/

articles/2014/12/31/3-steps-for-building-a-professional-learning.html.

Gaertner-Bridges, C. "Study Group Formation: Considerations and Guidelines." In *Financial Planning Study Group Considerations*. (n.d.) http://www.fpasv. org/wp-content/uploads/2013/12/Study_Group_Formation_Guidelines. pdf.

Greene, M. P. *Creative Mentorship and Career-Building Strategies: How to Build Your*

Virtual Personal Board of Directors. New York: Oxford University Press, 2015.

Grenny, J., and Han, V. "The Upside to Social Networking." *Chief Learning Officer*

10, no. 4 (April 2011): 30-33.

"How to Build Your Peer Learning Network When You "Don't Have Time." January 8, 2014. http://activatelearning.com.au/2014/01/how-to-build-your-peer-learning-network-when-you-dont-have-time/.

Koralesky, B., & Sparrow, J. "On the Shoulders of Giants: Leveraging Peer Networks for Leading-Edge Professional Development." *EDUCAUSE Review* 49, no. 1 (January 27, 2014).

Llopis, G. "7 Reasons Networking Can be a Professional Development Boot Camp." *Forbes*. 2012. http://www.forbes.com/sites/ glennllopis/2012/05/29/7-reasons-networking-can-be-a-professional-development-boot-camp/#61fad2ba1834.

Perle, J. "Networking: the Golden Rules." *Training Journal*. September 2015, 48-51.

"Tips for Successful Networking." *Sound & Video Contractor* 31, no. 9 (September 2013): 12.

Woods, B. Building Your Own PLN. *T+D* 67, no. 11 (2013): 70-73.

CHAPTER 6

Case Studies

Benefits of Case Studies for HR Competency Development

Case studies are a recognized and well-regarded learning tool and have these benefits for developing HR competencies:

- Building analytical skills by requiring participants to identify and describe the relevant problems or characteristics of the situation.

- Promoting problem-solving skills.

- Creating a safe, nonthreatening environment in that there is often no "right" or "wrong" answer and the benefit is in the discussion.

- Creating multiple layers of complexity, allowing the case to be useful to all levels of HR professionals.

- Using case studies is easy and they can be employed by one or more participants in a single or continuing series of discussions.

- Developing critical thinking and builds confidence.

- Finding them "off the shelf" or purposefully developed.

One of the best examples of experiential learning is the case study method. Contrary to the role-play method, which is a more direct way of learning, the case study method is a more classic approach to analyzing a problem, answering questions, and thinking about alternative solutions. The case study method can help HR professionals develop their analytical and problem-solving skills.

By presenting a story or a case about people, organizations, or situations that other HR professionals have faced, you create a story with which people can resonate. With cases there are many options. They can be based on real people, real organizations, real numbers, and real situations. Or they can be fictitious. A case can be made to be extreme or rather simplistic. Moreover, you can use existing case studies, develop them yourself, or ask others to do this for you.

The case study method is a form of experiential learning that fits the adult learner quite well in that it is a problem-based approach to learning. A case presents a situation or problem that could be or has been encountered. It needs to sufficiently detail the situation in a "story" or vignette. It can range from a single incident or problem to a scenario that takes place over a period of time. A case can be discussed or answered by an individual or a group. A common denominator in any case is that it requires the reader to think critically and then to develop a solution or set of responses. Cases can be driven by the context of a situation or by facts—or by both. They should be relatively recent to drive relevancy, and they should create empathy or mindfulness for the reader to enhance learning effectiveness. Case studies allow readers and participants to explore different angles and to challenge conventional or previous thinking.

To be effective, the description of an actual or made-up case must present an opportunity for the user to practice both diagnosing and solving a problem. A case study is a nonthreatening way for people to rehearse how they might analyze and behave in a similar situation. Case studies also allow the reader to build on previous experience while at the same time address new areas or learn new concepts.[1] They also let learners develop their own conclusions and, hence, develop critical thinking that is reflective of the behaviors they might employ in addressing a situation. With a case study, you can hone your skills by:

- Considering the research or questions you might explore to assist you in developing a response.

- Thinking about similar situations with which you've dealt and whether you handled them well or if you should have acted differently.

- Discussing the issues with others.

- Thinking about how you've seen others handle a similar situation and identifying their strengths or weaknesses in solving the problem.

- Considering an array of responses that might be effective and even identifying those that will not be effective.

- Learning from others by hearing their approaches and ideas.

Cases that are close to your current work experiences and those that reflect aspirational situations are the best to use. If the case represents something you have done before or experience frequently with little difficulty, it may not be as developmental as one involving components new to you or ones you know will present you with a challenge.

So where do you find a case, and how do you approach analyzing it? Finding an effective case that will allow you to skip the step of preparing your own case is quite doable. Take a look at any HR or business management textbook, and you are likely to find cases of all types, length, and complexity. In addition, many casebooks have been published and are available to the general public and not exclusively used in educational classrooms. In addition, a number of case repositories offer cases for sale or for use by the public. Some of these include those found in Table 6.1.

TABLE 6.1 PUBLIC SOURCES FOR CASE STUDIES

Guidance: The following sites offer free cases and links to cases that might be helpful to you as you think about using case studies to help develop your HR behavioral competencies.

"Business Case Studies: Free Case Studies," University of British Columbia, April 16, 2016
http://guides.library.ubc.ca/businesscases/free

"Case Studies," Learning Edge, MIT Sloan School of Management, 2016
https://mitsloan.mit.edu/LearningEdge/Pages/Case-Studies.aspx

"Case Studies," *New York Times*, 2016
http://topics.nytimes.com/top/news/business/small-business/case-studies/index.html

"Case Studies," University of Chicago Library
http://guides.lib.uchicago.edu/case_studies

"Case Study Examples and Sample Case Studies," Free Case Study
https://freecasestudy.wordpress.com/

"Case Study," ManagementParadise.com
http://www.managementparadise.com/mba-projects/free-case-study-download/

"Find Business Cases," McMaster University, December 22, 2015
http://library.mcmaster.ca/find/business-cases

"Free Case Studies," *RFID Journal*
http://www.rfidjournal.com/free-case-studies

TABLE 6.1 PUBLIC SOURCES FOR CASE STUDIES
"Free Cases," Case Centre, 2016 *http://www.thecasecentre.org/educators/casemethod/resources/freecasesoverview*
"Free/Sample/Inspection Case Studies," IBS Case Development Centre *http://www.ibscdc.org/free-case-studies.asp*
Karen Schweiter, "Free Case Studies," About Education, April 30, 2015 *http://businessmajors.about.com/od/casestudies/tp/casestudysample.htm*
"Management Resources," IBS Center for Management Research, 2010 *http://www.icmrindia.org/free%20resources/casestudies/freesample.htm*
"MBA Case Study Analysis, Term Papers, Research Papers," FreeCaseStudySolutions.Com *http://freecasestudysolutions.com/*
"The Times 100 Free Downloadable Business Case Studies," Deans Talk, July 5, 2008 *http://www.deanstalk.net/deanstalk/2008/07/the-times-100-f.html*

In addition to the possible sources for cases mentioned in Table 6.1, one excellent source for cases is your peers or yourself. For example, you can form a partnership with one or more individuals and write case vignettes for each other that will provide both challenge and development. The peer can be another HR professional or someone in a different function. With your partner, agree on specific competencies you want to develop. Taking the partnership a step further, you may also consider working together to discuss your responses and how you would approach the case at hand. The next section discusses the components of cases, should you want to prepare them for yourself.

Writing Your Own Case

Conceiving and writing your own case can be an effective way to self-direct what you need to develop, and the process can be a developmental experience in and of itself. Writing your own case can be time-consuming and may or may not provide you with new "problems" to solve or discuss unless you are thoughtful in your approach. Overall, you want to have as much detail as necessary to provide discussion and mediating factors—but not too much detail so that the case is too complex or unmanageable. Be wary of embedding too many problems in the case as this could cause confusion or too much competition over possible solutions.

You want to be realistic but not hit too close to home, or your discussion and analysis could become too emotional or personal and less practical. The case does need to be authentic, but if it replicates too closely a scenario in which you were involved, it may lose some of the learning potential.

The best approach to preparing "homegrown" cases is to form a partnership or engage someone to assist by preparing or reviewing a case with you in mind. Offering to jointly prepare and then trade cases can be developmental for you as well as for a colleague or peer. As with role-playing, asking someone in HR is fine, but including someone from outside the function may be more challenging and developmental. Don't be shy about asking others to do this with you because they may also welcome the opportunity for development. More than one partner can be sought, and more than one alliance can be helpful to your development.

What to Include in a Case

There are number of things to include if you are writing a case, working with a partner to create cases, or even evaluating a publicly available case you may be reviewing for possible use.

Prepare case and learning objectives. Identify the HR competency or competencies you are targeting. Indicate the career level or levels the case should focus on. Learning objectives should clearly state the expected goal or outcome of the case in terms of which knowledge, skills, abilities, and other characteristics (KSAOs) will be developed or demonstrated. In a sense, learning objectives provide you with the "directions" you need for the case—as do developing questions for the case.

Include relevant facts and data. Use facts and data that will provide appropriate complexity for the case discussion or test analytical skills. These data are independent of the context data; they can include charts or details about sales and turnover, engagement scores, product or market changes, financial data, and so forth.

Set the context. A case usually picks up in the middle of the story, so setting the stage for understanding the background is important.

Size of organization: number of employees, revenue, and geographic dispersion of facilities and employees.

Location of problem: business unit, level of management or line location, and specific city, country, or region where the problem is centered.

Characters: case protagonists, roles, names, and titles of people in the organization, reporting relationships, etc.

Physical setting: plant, office, meeting, etc.

Sector: relevant facts such as collective bargaining agreements, partnerships, and contractual agreements.

Time frame issues: period the case takes place in and if the time frame affects issues for reaching a decision or conclusion. Other relevant demographic or factual details.

Include dialogue if possible. Dialogue helps bring more life to the case and creates the potential for empathy and mindfulness in the discussion. If the "problem" is a disagreement over strategies or even tactics, it might be helpful to demonstrate the two points of view through two or more characters exchanging ideas or opinions.

Include a list of specific discussion questions. The questions should be relevant to the story and flow from your learning objectives and from the data provided in the case. They should be as specific as possible. Also use the list of generic questions provided above.

Obtain feedback. Before finalizing the case, ask someone else to read and test the case for usefulness. This input can be a learning experience in and of itself. For example, if a reviewer asks about missing data or comments that some data are irrelevant, this information can be insightful. Feedback, as a way to obtain constructive criticism, can be helpful in developing a case that will be more realistic and a superior learning tool. Incorporate feedback and revise accordingly.

Generate variations. Prepare subsections that are relevant to different career levels (entry, mid, senior, and executive) or to different roles (for example, HR generalist, HR specialist in recruiting or compensation, HR business partner, HR line manager).

Create a template. You can use the template to easily create cases in the future. Templates are guides that help you organize your thoughts and bring structure to the exercise. By using a template, you may be able to provide all the information you need without having to prepare a lot of narrative. This can help save you time. Table 6.2 provides an example of a case writing template.

TABLE 6.2 CASE STUDY TEMPLATE FOR PREPARING AN ORIGINAL CASE

Case study objective:

HR competencies intended to develop:

Learning objectives:

Context:

    Size of organization:

    Location of problem:

    Characters:

    Physical setting:

    Sector:

    Time frame issues:

    Other relevant facts:

Dialogue options:

Specific case discussion questions:

Feedback received:

Variations:

Instructions: Provide as much detail as possible or that is needed to facilitate rich discussion and analysis.

TABLE 6.3 QUESTIONS TO USE WITH ANY CASE TO GUIDE LEARNING EXERCISE

What behaviors did you notice that were affected in the case? Identify the affected behaviors, and be specific as to who displayed them. As appropriate, discuss this with another person to confirm or explore differences.

Notes:

_____

_____

_____

What is the overarching problem? What are the sub-elements of the problem, and how would you prioritize them?

Notes:

_____

_____

_____

What actions do you recommend taking to address the problem? What are the pros and cons of each of your recommended actions?

Notes:

_____

_____

_____

What are the likely reactions (by characters in the case) to your recommendations?

Notes:

_____

_____

_____

What did you learn about analyzing a problem and your own behaviors by reading this case? What can you apply right now in your personal sphere?

Notes:

_____

_____

_____

What did you learn about each HR behavioral competency? Run down the list of each of the eight behavioral competencies, determine which ones apply and note any relevant ideas or behavioral implications for each.

Notes:

_____

_____

_____

TABLE 6.3 QUESTIONS TO USE WITH ANY CASE TO GUIDE LEARNING EXERCISE
How will you use the knowledge and skills you've encountered in the case in the future? Be specific and identify a range of possible applications.   Notes:
What helped or hindered your analysis of the people, problems, or organization in this case?   Notes:
What facts or behaviors were seemingly small at first read but which turned out to play a key role?   Notes:
Are there other questions that you think may be helpful to add to this list?   Notes:

Coaching Tip

As an HR leader, you may have insight about potential changes that will occur in the HR function or the organization, or you may have the desire for a particular new initiative for the team. You can provide some basic ideas and then ask HR staff to prepare various case vignettes to address the issues or subsets of the issues. You can conduct individual or group discussions about the case vignettes. This approach can help your staff members develop their competencies and prepare them for situations potentially on their horizon.

The two cases below are offered as examples of cases that can be prepared and that target specific HR competencies. Note that using the suggested template is not necessary as long as the key features are included. These cases provide the context and the description, offer variations by level, and provide detailed questions specific to each variation. In addition to developing questions specific to any case, also keep in mind a general set of questions that can guide the learning experience. Table 6.3 provides a list of such questions.

Case Study by Level

Level differences with respect to using a case for learning purposes can be addressed by the depth of the case and the complexity of the questions. The common denominator in a case is problem-solving and discussing solutions to problems, conflict, or business dilemmas. A good case study makes the participant think critically about the data and details presented. As a result, you can provide different aspects of a case and create different levels of complexity.

At the *entry level*, a case may focus more on identifying the problem and exploring what data and information are needed to begin to solve the problem. The case may not provide many layers of data, and it may not include a large number of characters or collateral issues. An entry-level case is also an opportunity to introduce additional functional HR issues and to focus on behavioral competencies. Exposure to a variety of HR issues can help build critical thinking and other behavioral competencies while at the same time expand the parameters of what an HR professional knows.

At the *mid level*, additional assumptions can be made about what the HR professional knows or has had experience with, and this enables you to develop or use a case that has more detail and intricacy with respect to the problems and the intersection of problems. The case may raise a more thought-provoking issue or present a more difficult conflict to be addressed. The case should be concise but provide more information about characters and greater contextual detail than at the entry level. Participants may have an opportunity to use additional analytical tools in problem-solving and to apply and develop their skills more fully.

At the *senior level*, the complexity can grow even more, and cases may entail the participant needing to take more of a stand or a position. This may provide an opportunity for debate. One way to accomplish this is by using a case that creates some decision points for the characters in the case and, hence, the participant. There may be multiple problems that intersect and a cascading effect that earlier decisions have on the discussion of other parts of the case. The more complications, the greater the challenge and the greater likelihood that participants will not all take the same position or approach the analysis in the same way. There is not likely to be a clear-cut answer, and if developed well, the case can build a scenario in which empathy is part of the mix, which may create more complication and, hence, a greater learning experience.

At the *executive level*, it may be more fruitful to look at the case as a way to build your HR team and provide opportunities for HR professionals at all levels to learn from others. At the executive level, it is not likely that you will need a case to help you build your competency unless the case is in a different business discipline and the objective is to build your competency for critical thinking in another discipline, such as finance or marketing. At this level, selecting or building a case based on your expertise can drive learning and development because it will be based on accumulated knowledge of critical HR issues in a problem-solving context. One recommendation is to be sure to cover a variety of HR behavioral competencies rather than homing in on just one or two.

Case Study Example 1: Communication HR Competency[2]

Case Vignette

Layoffs are an unfortunate but often necessary means of conducting business. Quite frequently, employers will go to great lengths to avoid eliminating jobs, but ultimately must reduce the size of their payrolls for their businesses to succeed going forward.

This is the scenario faced by Triple A Retail, a seller of clothes and home goods. What began as a small family operation 60 years ago has grown into a regional enterprise with 12 locations and 400 employees in six states, but increased competition from national corporations and Internet-based retailers has taken a toll on Triple A's sales in recent months.

To date, Triple A's executive team has enacted several cost-cutting measures without conducting layoffs. The moves have included increasing employees' share of contributions to health care coverage, eliminating employee discounts on Triple A Retail merchandise, and reducing the payout level of annual bonuses by 50 percent.

These measures have helped cut expenses, but they have also created concern among the employee ranks. Rumors of layoffs, store closures, and other sizable reductions have begun to circulate, and morale is at extremely low levels, based on anecdotal conversations between HR representatives and workers at the company's 12 stores.

The executive team is, in fact, preparing for a potential overhaul of the business that will essentially cut its operations in half. It calls for the closure of six stores and the elimination of nearly 200 jobs, but it comes with a caveat—the moves won't be necessary if the company makes its sales goals this year, and these goals hinge on the success of a new product that it recently launched and made available in its stores.

Entry level

No matter what occurs, employees are already on edge. You are an HR generalist at Triple A Retail, and you have been charged with supporting the HR director in an internal communications campaign that will address the recent cuts and the proposed changes to the business if it fails to meet its sales goals.

1. How will this message be disseminated among employees, and what will be your role?
2. Have you talked about these issues yet with employees, and if so, have you shared the results of those conversations with the HR director?
3. How will you address this situation with new employees at Triple A Retail?
4. Are there any internal or external resources that may help you as you support the HR director in this endeavor?
5. Have you considered the sensitive nature of this topic and what level of discretion you will use when relaying any information to employees?

Mid level

No matter what occurs, employees are already on edge. You are a mid-level HR professional at Triple A Retail, and you have been charged with supporting the HR director in an internal communications campaign that will address the recent cuts and the proposed changes to the business if it fails to meet its sales goals.

1. Based on what you have heard from employees, have you shared this information with senior management? If so, how will it affect the development of this communications campaign?
2. What type of assistance will you request from your support staff in human resources?
3. Given the sensitive nature of this topic, what level of discretion will you use when relaying this information to your HR support staff?
4. What type of internal resources will you use to disseminate this information to employees?
5. Have you considered a social media strategy for this effort, in case any of this information becomes public?

Senior level

No matter what occurs, employees are already on edge. You are the HR director at Triple A Retail, and you have been charged with overseeing an internal communications campaign that will address the recent cuts and proposed changes to the business if it fails to meet sales goals.

1. Before this plan is finalized, have you considered addressing the employees in the interim? Is there any benefit to informing them that they will soon be fully apprised of the company's situation?
2. What type of assistance will you request from your support staff and managers in human resources in this endeavor?
3. Are there any external resources that you can draw on while overseeing the development of this communications campaign? Have similar situations occurred elsewhere that may provide some guidance?
4. How will you deliver this information to the leaders of other business units at Triple A Retail?
5. What is your timeline for delivering this proposal to the chief HR officer (CHRO)?

Executive level

No matter what occurs, employees are already on edge. You are the CHRO at Triple A Retail, and you have been charged with approving an internal communications campaign that will address the recent cuts and the proposed changes to the business if it fails to meet its sales goals. You will also determine how this information will be disseminated to the public, if the company does not reach those sales goals.

1. Whose feedback will you solicit before you approve this plan?
2. How will this plan be disseminated to employees?
3. Will there be any safeguards or measures taken to ensure that this information does not become public?
4. If this information does become public, how do you plan to address this with customers or with the media?
5. If the company reaches its sales goals and this restructuring plan is ultimately not necessary, have you considered how to improve communications with employees to avoid a similar situation in the future?

Case Study Example 2: Business Acumen HR Competency[3]

Case Vignette

Wethersfield Quality Materials is a small manufacturer that makes components for electrical systems. The company has had modest revenues for most of its existence but lately has seen increased demand for its products, and sales have risen steadily for the past several months.

Wethersfield Quality Materials derives the bulk of its sales from electrical systems installed in commercial and residential buildings, and forecasts from the construction industry have called for real estate development to increase sharply for the next several years. These circumstances have presented the company with an opportunity to expand its operations for the long term.

To date, the company has asked its nonexempt employees to work extra hours to meet the demand for production, but the CEO has determined that this is not sustainable, and she would like to hire additional staff. The company needs welders, electronic assemblers, and engineers, but workers with these skill sets are in short supply in the market surrounding Wethersfield Quality Materials' operations.

The manufacturing sector overall has struggled to find qualified candidates for its job openings, and this has hampered productivity in the industry. Several research publications have reinforced this trend: Reports from the Society for

Human Resource Management, for example, show that recruiting difficulty is at historically high levels in the manufacturing industry.

Another area of concern at Wethersfield Quality Materials is the aging of its workforce. Several of its employees will be eligible to retire in the next three to five years, at a time when demand for the company's products could be at its height. This trend is not unique to the company—the U.S. labor force overall is getting older, which has forced many employers to reevaluate their recruiting and retention strategies.

Entry level

You have recently been hired as an HR generalist at Wethersfield Quality Materials. You have been charged with supporting the HR director in the development of a staffing management plan that will address the current and future needs of its workforce.

1. What is your first course of action?
2. What external or internal resources might you use to address this issue?
3. Are there any data or research from the government or private sector that may be helpful to you?
4. If there is a budget for this endeavor, how would you determine the cost-benefit analysis?
5. What are your deadlines for providing support materials to the HR director?

Mid level

You are a mid-level HR professional at Wethersfield Quality Materials. You have been charged with assisting the executive team in the development of a staffing management plan that will address the current and future needs of the organization's workforce.

1. What are the business units at your organization, and how will they be affected by this plan?
2. What internal or external resources are available that will help you develop this plan?
3. What is the budget for this plan?
4. Are there any metrics, data, or related research that will help you develop this plan?

5. How will the staffing shortage affect the organization's marketing strategy? Are there ways to promote the organization that may make it appear more attractive to prospective job candidates?

Senior level

You are a senior-level HR professional at Wethersfield Quality Materials. You have been charged with developing a staffing management plan that will address the current and future needs of its workforce.

1. Knowing that workers with these skills are in short supply, what external resources might you use to address this issue?
2. What internal resources are available to help you address this issue in the short term?
3. Do you have specific benchmarks (for example, the number of workers needed to handle the forecasted increase in production) that you can use to help you develop your staffing management strategy?
4. Knowing that the workforce is aging, both internally and externally, how might this affect the retention element of your strategy? The recruiting element?
5. How will this strategy affect the organization's bottom line?
6. How will you present this strategy to the organization's HR executive?

Executive level

You are an executive-level HR professional at Wethersfield Quality Materials. Your HR team has developed a staffing management plan that will address the current and future needs of the company's workforce, and it has been sent to you for your review.

- What is the business case for this issue?
- Are there any government initiatives (for example, workforce development programs) in your region that may align with this plan, and if so, how will you use them to support this effort?
- How will this strategy affect the organization's bottom line?
- What are the benefits and risks of this plan as it has been presented to you? What is the return on investment (ROI), and is it aligned with the organization's broader strategic plan?

- How will you present this strategy to the rest of the executive team and to the other employees in the organization?

Chapter Summary

- Case studies are a nonthreatening way for HR professionals to build problem-solving skills and confidence in confronting problems.

- Cases cover situations that HR professionals have dealt with or may deal with in the future.

- Writing your own case and partnering with others can be an effective approach.

- Cases, whether you write them or obtain them from an outside source, should include some specific components to obtain the greatest benefit from the exercise.

- Case studies enhance learning through the application of knowledge and can facilitate rapid understanding and workplace understanding.

- Cases allow participants to arrive at their own conclusions—which might differ from the conclusions of others, depending on the size of the organization, the industry, and the location.

Additional Resources for Effective Case Studies

Barbazette, J. *Instant Case Studies: How to Design, Adapt, and Use Case Studies in Training.* San Francisco: Pfeiffer, 2004.

Iannarino, A. "Write Your Own Success (and Failure) Case Studies." *The Sales Blog.* May 23, 2013. http://thesalesblog.com/blog/2010/05/23/write-your-own-success-and-failure-case-studies/.

Mind Tools. "Case Study-Based Learning: Enhancing Learning through Immediate Application." (n.d.). https://www.mindtools.com/pages/article/newISS_94.htm.

Naumes, W., and Naumes, M. J. *The Art & Craft of Case Writing*, 3rd ed. Armonk, NY: M.E. Sharpe, 2012.

Richard Ivey School of Business Foundation. "Teaching & Authoring Tools: Authoring Tips & Tricks." (n.d.). https://www.iveycases.com/TeachingAuthoringTools.aspx.

Society for Human Resource Management. SHRM Learning Resources:

Case Study Student Workbooks. (n.d.). www.shrm.org/communities/studentprograms/pages/default.aspx.

Vega, G. *The Case Writing Workbook: A Self-Guided Workshop*. London: Routledge, 2015.

Purposeful Discussion

Benefits of Purposeful Discussion for HR Competency Development

Interactive discussions that have an intended purpose allow for many benefits:
- Learning valuable information from others.
- Understanding others' motivations and insights.
- Building confidence.
- Improving execution in stating ideas.
- Gaining perspective on what is competent behavior and what is not.
- Building relationships.
- Practicing being better understood.
- Gaining insight into yourself.

The Socratic method is often thought of as a form of teaching or as a teaching tactic. It can be a powerful method for directing the learner toward critical thinking. The leader of the dialogue in the Socratic method asks probing questions with the objective being critical thought—typically in the area of values, beliefs, and principles. And while Socrates focused on moral education, HR professionals can apply this method to learning more about themselves and critically evaluating knowledge, skills, abilities, and other characteristics (KSAOs) as well as developing KSAOs based on the evaluation. To this end, let's consider how to have *purposeful discussion* that leads to learning and understanding which behaviors are successful in which circumstances and which may be less successful. Asking questions can lead to greater understanding of a person's actions in a given context and of which behaviors may be more effective than others. Responses to questions can provide awareness of options to be employed in similar situations. If we are to learn from others' behaviors and actions and to develop our own behaviors and actions, we need to know how to process and filter the information. One way to do this is by asking better questions and by being systematic in how we approach asking questions and engaging in discussions.

The philosopher Voltaire said it best: "Judge a man by his questions rather than by his answers."[1] Martial arts expert Bruce Lee extended this by saying, "A wise man can learn more from a foolish question than a fool can learn from a wise question."[2] The focus in this chapter is on questions and dialogue for the purpose of developing HR competencies overall. If one can learn by asking and by doing, then getting better at asking and dialoguing can provide a greater return. Questions, asked in the right way, can stimulate thinking on the part of both the respondent and the inquirer.

Getting Started

First, think about what you are trying to accomplish or what you want to gain by asking your questions and engaging in dialogue. Go back to your self-assessment and consider what areas you need to develop and which ones may be well suited to questions and discussion. For example, if you would like to build your ability to develop relationships at the executive level, then you need to pose your questions in a way that will provide you with the vision and perception of how you should behave in the future. Or if you want to build your global and cultural effectiveness, then you may take a different approach. Here are a few things to think about in forming your questions.

Avoid Categorical Questions

For competency development purposes, try not to ask simple yes or no questions. As a rule, you will likely receive less complete or insightful responses. For example, "Have you been developing a relationship with this insurance vendor for a long time?" versus "How long have you been developing the relationship with this vendor, and what has been most effective in developing the relationship?" Or "Have you traveled to China on business before?" versus "What have been your experiences in traveling to China, and what are some important things to know?"

Probe

Have a follow-up question ready. In some situations, you may be looking for factual information, and probing may or may not be necessary. But if you're asking questions for the purpose of building your competencies and creating a dialogue rather than as part of a routine inquiry, then you want someone else's keen understanding and perception. For instance, you can follow up with a specific question about the response, or ask "What makes you *say* that?" or "What makes you *think* that?" The reason for asking a probing follow-up question is not simply to take on someone else's opinion or view; it will help you develop your own sentiment or conviction that is based on hearing a variety of viewpoints. For example, "How does this insurance vendor compare with other insurance brokers you've dealt with in the past?" Or "Yes, I've heard that following protocol is highly valued in China—was there anything in particular that one should avoid doing?"

Zip Your Lip

Silence can be uncomfortable, but it can also be potent. If someone does not answer right away, wait for a response. If the answer is short, wait for someone to say more by looking a bit quizzical. The person you're talking to may have a lot more to say and will bring it out if you wait patiently. Often people feel compelled to fill in the silence and may provide more critical insight if you do not say anything.

Listen Intently and Do Not Interrupt

The people with whom you are speaking want to be valued. They are more likely to keep talking if they feel valued by you. Moreover, you do not want to risk any distraction—particularly if they are describing a behavior or their motivation behind a behavior. If they happen to be conveying something you already know (about insurance vendors or China, for example), let this be a repetition for you and nod encouragingly as you think of a probing follow-up questions. Which

HR behavioral competency you're focusing on may also make a difference. For example, if you are dialoguing with someone with the intent to learn about leadership and navigation, then letting the person talk in an open way may be more insightful with respect to how he or she approaches the situation versus if you ask more, or leading, questions.

Ask the Right Kinds of Questions

Make sure that your questions fit the situation. A question in and of itself may not be inappropriate, but it may not be the right question in a given context. For example, if you are discussing an ethical dilemma with a colleague, asking about someone else's ethical behavior may be inappropriate. In addition, you should ask questions that empower the respondent to answer in a forthright and helpful manner, such as "I value your views on HR in China since you have traveled there and I have not—what was your biggest surprise, either positive or negative?"

Don't Be Afraid of the Answer You Might Receive

If you're asking a question about a vendor or trying to understand why a colleague handled a situation in a particular way, there's not much to fear, and you can may gain some interesting ideas about how you might behave in the future. For instance, "My last experience engaging an insurance broker was a bit of a disaster. Apparently I asked a question she found insulting; how can I avoid something like that in the future?"

Get Personal

Don't be afraid to get personal and ask for specific feedback. For example, you might ask a colleague, supervisor, or even a subordinate, "How do you think I could have handled that situation differently?" Don't ask "How did I do?" because it does not open the door wide enough for feedback. After explaining something, ask "Have I been clear? (rather than "Do you understand?") Did I explain my interaction with the insurance broker sufficiently? I must've done something to elicit that response." Often, the more specific you can be, the better.

Be a Leader

The use of questions or dialogue can also be a way to help others and to create mutually beneficial exchanges. Be open to questions that you receive. If someone asks you about an insurance broker, you may actually find your response to be insightful. Responding why you found one better than another may actually help you articulate something you had not thought of previously. Displaying your own expertise in a dialogue with responses to questions can be enlightening.

Questions for Purposeful Discussion

Along with these general tips, see the sample questions in Tables 7.1 and 7.2. The former provides general questions for engaging in purposeful dialogue to develop competencies, and the latter provides specific questions relating to each behavioral competency. You can take these questions and use them to help boost a dialogue in which you are trying to develop your own behavioral competencies. You may also take these questions and modify them to tailor the discussion to a specific HR competency.

TABLE 7.1 GENERAL QUESTIONS

Socratic Method—Purposeful Discussion: These are general questions. You can use these questions for yourself in any number of situations and may use the same questions in more than one setting or situation. For specific questions by behavioral competency, see Table 7.2.

What do you hope to gain by using that strategy? Why did you select that strategy?
Notes:

_____

_____

_____

From your perspective, is that a tactic or a strategy? When is it appropriate to call something a strategy versus a tactic? Are these words sometimes used interchangeably?
Notes:

_____

_____

_____

How would you prioritize _____ and why?
Notes:

_____

_____

_____

TABLE 7.1 GENERAL QUESTIONS

Is there another way we could say this that might be clearer?
Notes:

_____

_____

_____

Help me understand why . . .
Notes:

_____

_____

_____

That's interesting. Can you also consider _____ as a possibility?
Notes:

_____

_____

_____

Nonverbal communication often accounts for additional messages. Is there something I do that may be off-putting? What mannerisms do I need to monitor? What mannerisms do I have that are effective?
Notes:

_____

_____

_____

I understand your point of view. Can you explain this aspect a bit more?
Notes:

_____

_____

_____

Why did you increase your budget in _____ area?
Notes:

_____

_____

_____

What additional questions can you think of to add to this list?
Notes:

_____

_____

_____

TABLE 7.2 SAMPLE QUESTIONS TO USE TO DEVELOP YOUR HR COMPETENCIES

Instructions: Keep some of these questions at the ready and consider asking them randomly or systematically. If randomly, ask one or more questions when you want to affect your own behavior or understand someone else's behavior. If systematically, select an issue or specific behavior, and ask the same question of multiple people from multiple positions or orientations. Either approach can be used regularly. Take notes or log the responses so you can go back and envision the possible impact the range of responses can have on you and your behavior.

Business Acumen

- What are the publications or websites I should read on a consistent basis to learn more about _____ industry?
- Where is our organization expanding, and what aspects of the economy will affect our business?
- What business scenarios are we likely to face in the next 6 to 12 months?
- How does our business make money? Certainly sales are important, but how do we account for our overall financial success?
- What's the big picture for our organization in the next three to five years, and what will be the key drivers of our success?

Communication

- In your view, what are some of the keys to crafting effective messages?
- How can we tailor messages to various audiences and levels to communicate effectively?
- Which media do you think are the best communication methods—and for which audiences?
- What are the keys to your effective listening skills when dealing with employee relations issues or when working with outside parties?

Consultation

- How do you conduct initial investigations of HR issues?
- How do you coach line managers on investigating HR issues?
- How do you coach line managers on dealing with HR issues?
- What approach do you use to supervise HR issues?
- How do you interact with legal counsel when dealing with an HR issue?

Critical Evaluation

- What qualitative information do you seek to help you analyze and interpret key HR initiatives? What quantitative data do you seek?
- What are some examples of how you've used data to make a business case for a decision or recommendation you were hoping to have accepted?
- I'm familiar with basic statistics, but what else do I need to know to evaluate and support HR initiatives?
- What sorts of data resonate more with managers at different levels? How do you know what the best approach will be for different groups?
- Does evidence-based information need to come from just inside our organization, or are there credible ways to use outside resources to support initiatives?

TABLE 7.2 SAMPLE QUESTIONS TO USE TO DEVELOP YOUR HR COMPETENCIES

Ethical Practice

- From your perspective, what does it look like when someone maintains a high level of personal and professional integrity?
- How do you demonstrate ethical behavior throughout the organization? What resonates the most with employees at different levels?
- How do you balance transparency and confidentiality? Are the two sometimes in conflict?
- How do you help other executives see and identify any biases they might have?

Global and Cultural Effectiveness

- What has been the most interesting or most difficult experience you've had in dealing with cultural differences?
- What were one or two things you would have done differently?
- What was the most effective way of handling the situation—and why?
- What are some of the key things you can tell me about [China, India, the Muslim culture, LGBT issues] in your organization?
- How are diversity and inclusion handled in your organization?
- Would you modify your approach if you could?
- How much of your role focuses on global activities, and how have you developed your expertise in this area?

Leadership and Navigation

- When rolling out a new HR policy, how do you demonstrate flexibility?
- What steps do you take when pushing a timeline for a new policy?
- How do you ensure alignment between your HR vision and your organization's strategy?
- What does it look like when you champion the HR function inside your organization?

Relationship Management

- What techniques do you use to build effective and lasting relationships with others, and how do these techniques differ, if at all, with contacts inside the organization compared with outside the organization?
- What are some ways you leverage your relationships to learn more about best practices or how certain implementation efforts are working?
- How do you express concern about the well-being of employees and colleagues without getting too personal?
- What are some of the more difficult conflicts you've had to deal with, and how did you resolve them? Is there a common denominator in your approach?

Coaching Tip

In an HR staff meeting, tell your staff members that you will begin using the Socratic method or simply that you want to have more purposeful dialogue. Challenge them to each ask at least one question per meeting for the purpose of their own development, rather than just for addressing the business at hand in the meeting. Another option would be to hold a purposeful discussion of each HR behavioral competency on a monthly basis. Have all your staff, at all levels, come to a meeting or discussion hour with the intent of talking about what business acumen and critical evaluation look like in your organization—what the proficient behaviors are and why. You can use the descriptions in the SHRM Competency Model (see Appendix B), or you can ask people to define or describe their own applications. Using the questions in Table 7.1 is also an option

Conversation is an interactive activity and represents a more spontaneous communication—even if it occurs in a scheduled meeting. Conversation or discussion can occur between two or more people. You can pose a question to one person at a time or to multiple people. The development of questioning and discussion skills can facilitate learning and the formation of behaviors. While conversation may occur informally and be more general, you can have a chat or discussion with someone about specific topics, and you can direct it with purposeful intent. An exchange or shooting the breeze may occur throughout the day, but when it is done with purpose, it may take on a more significant meaning for you and may be a source of learning and development.

Typically, a question is used to evoke a response to draw out information from the person or persons being addressed. This differs in purpose from asking a question to test someone or to guide a discussion. There are many different types of questions. For example, surveys and personal exchanges may have open- or closed-ended questions. The questions can be categorized as descriptive, relational, causal, rhetorical, philosophical, or even loaded![3] For the purpose of developing your HR competencies, you're not likely to use loaded or rhetorical questions. However, descriptive, relational, and causal questions may all be quite useful. Descriptive questions are used to gather information about someone or something, whereas relational questions explore relationships between two or more people or variables. For instance, how does insurance broker A compare with insurance broker B? With causal questions, the purpose is to ascertain if something affects something else—does one variable influence the outcome of the other variables. For instance, "Do business protocols in China influence when and how meetings take place?" Philosophical questions may be used to reflect on certain situations that you are uncertain about or that arise when dealing with practical issues—they may even border on strategic issues: "Should we match, lead, or lag the market with respect to a base salary approach?"

Table 7.3 provides some suggestions for how to be more confident while engaging in dialogue. The statements may come after a question has been posed. The point is that dialogue takes effort. Since it involves at least two people, if you are to take the initiative to have this be a developmental dialogue, it may be helpful to use transitional phrases or effective ways to continue the dialogue. For example, an effective transitional statement might be "I see your point. May I ask you another question?" or "Can we back up a second? I'm not sure I follow the logic on your last point."

TABLE 7.3 PHRASES TO FACILITATE DISCUSSION

Phrases to use to be confident in stating a position or starting a discussion for learning.

- Let's step back for a second and . . .
- I don't think I've been clear . . .
- Thank you for that explanation—may I ask a few more questions . . .
- That being said, can we also . . .
- I see your point . . .
- With all due respect, I'm not sure I agree . . .
- As a practical matter . . .
- I'm not opposed to your position; however, . . .
- I agree with you—and . . .
- I don't disagree—but/and . . .
- The next point I'd like to make . . .
- Now that we've established . . .
- Keeping these points in mind . . .
- Contrast that with . . .
- Can you clarify what you mean by . . .
- As you can see from these examples, . . .
- My first point is . . .
- Most convincingly . . .

Nonverbal Communication in Discussions

Nonverbal communication accounts for the majority of messages communicated between individuals. Although what we say or ask is important, it is often the way we say it or ask it that speaks volumes. Our tone, facial expressions, whether we make eye contact, gestures, and even our stance or posture often communicate as much, if not more than, the words we use. We must be mindful of all the cues we send when attempting dialogue and asking purposeful questions. Individuals with whom we communicate or target for purposeful discussion interpret all of our cues, possibly influencing the responses or reception we receive. When we ask questions, we are encoding a message to someone. When we interpret the questions (or the response), we are decoding the message.[4]

If your purpose is to gain development, then your interaction should be face-to-face rather than over e-mail or telephone. Face-to-face means that nonverbal communication will definitely come into play. The following are a few tips to keep in mind when you are planning for purposeful discussion. They apply to all HR professionals, but they are especially relevant for entry- or mid-level career professionals. Understanding these factors and applying this knowledge to your behavior can not only help you with learning and developing strong HR behavioral competencies, but they can also help with overall career development.

Appearance

If your purposeful discussion is with someone more senior or outside of your immediate area, or with someone you do not know or know well, be thoughtful about what would be professionally appropriate to wear for the exchange. You are the ultimate judge as to what is appropriate, but do *think* about it, and don't assume that your appearance is irrelevant.

Eye Contact

Even if you are nervous or feel uncomfortable, because you do or don't know the individual, make eye contact. This will communicate your sincerity and interest in the individual's response. Eye contact is especially meaningful in face-to-face conversations because it helps establish a flow to the conversation and helps you gauge the other person's reaction and response.

Facial Expressions

Whether we intend them to be or not, our faces are usually quite expressive. The face can communicate emotions, confusion, and much more while speaking or even when you are silent. It is not usually possible to hide our emotions or our interpretations. However, be mindful of extreme expressions that may communicate something you did not intend. And pay close attention to the expressions of the person you are speaking with to judge whether you have been understood or misunderstood.

Gestures and Posture

Gestures are a common occurrence in everyday life, and while some of us use more gestures than others, we should be cautious about what we are communicating. This is particularly true across cultures. The way we physically move or carry ourselves conveys meaning or indicates what we think or feel. Keep a professional demeanor at all times, particularly if it is someone with whom you are less familiar or with whom you have only a professional relationship.

Space

Be cognizant of where you are standing or sitting and where the other person is standing or sitting. Space can create a comfortable exchange—or sometimes an uncomfortable one if you are standing either too close or too far away. The need for space or distance varies for each person and certainly across cultures.

Voice and Tone

You've undoubtedly heard the saying "It's not just what you say, but how you say it." People will interpret what you say and the questions you ask by both your words and tone. Consider the speed, timing, volume, and inflections you use. In addition, think about how smoothly you deliver both questions and answers, and be cognizant of your use of "um" or "ah" or other fillers.

Coaching Tip

HR professionals should be seen as confident in addition to being competent. Confidence is often demonstrated in nonverbal behaviors. Having senior staff work with entry- and mid-level HR professionals to help them see and understand this can be valuable from a developmental perspective.

Purposeful Questions and Discussion by Level

We all ask questions just about every day and throughout the day. Questions almost always have a purpose—even if they are just rhetorical. But purposeful questions or discussions are more deliberate and intentional. In the case of using this approach for developing HR competencies, you could even say that their use is more calculated or premeditated. HR professionals at all levels can consciously use this approach to build their confidence and to assess competencies in others.

At the *entry level*, HR professionals, using the learning approach described in this chapter, can expand their knowledge and also begin to determine where gaps in both knowledge and behavior may exist. Entry-level HR professionals should seek out a wide variety of people and levels with which to engage and target questions and discussions appropriately. At the entry level, purposeful discussion can serve a variety of purposes. It is a learning activity to be sure, but it can also be coupled with networking, observation, case study, and so much more. Conscious inquiry is a good skill to have not just in personal development, but in professional success overall.

At the *mid level*, HR professionals should continue focusing on gaining knowledge and looking for gaps in their competencies. However, they also need to have a broader view and incorporate more specific projects or assignments on which they are working in order to build their competencies. This may even mean seeking out certain individuals, or certain types of individuals, or situations that connect to your work. Engaging in purposeful discussion may also be a way to become recognized as a professional who wants to learn, develop, and advance.

At the *senior level*, because you're more experienced, you want to add some additional focus and direction dependent on your own position and career aspirations. At this level you're more likely to be developing plans or leading the implementation of a development plan and will be more likely interested in causal relationship questions. Your discussions and the questions you plan are likely to be more specific and in-depth, and consist of exchange or sharing of opinions versus more general discourse. Your purpose is different and more focused as a result the experience can be generally developmental.

Finally, at the *executive level*, your purposeful discussion and questions are as likely to be an evaluation of your staff as they are for general development. Although your executive competencies may be well developed, and you may have little need for career development, there is still a need to be self-aware and to challenge what you know. For example, seasoned HR executives might find a need to expand their KSAOs if their company is broadening its geographic reach or expanding its products into new or related industries. The discussion questions and purpose behind them may change as HR professionals move to successively higher levels, but the need for and value of these exchanges will not disappear.

Purposeful discussions and questions should be planned in advance and approached with intent. However, the concept of using questions and discussions should be at the ready to be used anywhere and anytime. As with networking (see Chapter 5) in which you might find yourself seated next to a chief HR officer (CHRO) on an airplane or at an event, you never know when an opportunity may present itself. Be ready with your purposeful questions and take advantage of situations as they become available. Unlike networking, a purposeful discussion or question does not require the objective of building a long-term relationship.

Chapter Summary

- Asking questions in a way to promote dialogue helps HR professionals obtain greater return on their time investment in developing HR competencies.
- Forming your questions should be a formal and thoughtful process.
- Nonverbal communication can have a major influence on dialogue and discussion.
- Purposeful discussion enables the individual to gain perspective and to practice dialogue skills and grow abilities.

Additional Resources for Purposeful Discussion

Barkley, E., Cross, K., and Major, C. (2005). *Collaborative Learning Techniques*. San Francisco: Jossey-Bass, 2005.

Brookfield, S., and Preskill, S. *Discussion as a Way of Teaching: Tools and Techniques for Democratic Classrooms*, 2nd ed. San Francisco: Jossey-Bass, 2005.

Center for Teaching and Learning Stanford University. "The Socratic Method: What It Is and How to Use It in the Classroom." *Speaking of Teaching*. Fall 2003.

Knapp, M., Hall, J., and Horgan, T. *Nonverbal Communication in Human Interaction*, 8th ed. Boston: Wadsworth Cengage, 2014.

Ross, J. "How to Ask Better Questions." Harvard Business Review. 2009. https://hbr.org/2009/05/real-leaders-ask.php.

CHAPTER 8 Purposeful Observation

Benefits of Purposeful Observation for HR Competency Development

Watching the behavior of others with purposeful intent provides numerous benefits for HR competency development:

- Opportunity to learn and absorb in a nonobvious way.

- Freedom to learn from those whom you may not have comfort in approaching directly.

- Chance to test some ideas about what might work in one situation versus another situation.

- Social learning, which can take place anywhere at any time.

- Opportunity for behavioral modeling without the structure of a role-play.

- Chance to see both positive and negative examples of behaviors that influence your competence and the way you are perceived.

Observation involves careful watching or listening. It is the art of paying attention, with purpose, to someone or something to gain insight or information. Purposeful observation can serve professionals well if they are trying to develop their own skills. Observation can be formal or informal and can be driven by one's job or simply of one's own volition. For example, observation is part of the job of police officers. They are trained to watch for problems or issues of safety. Other people, however, may not have specific training or consider observation part of their job or realize that purposeful observation can help them develop skills and behaviors that will be valuable in the future. Like police officers who can prevent or resolve problems with their careful observational skills, HR professionals can have a positive influence through careful observation.

Observation involves taking note of certain facts or behaviors and recognizing patterns—or the lack of patterns. It may involve mental or written note-taking. And it can involve measuring or recording certain things such as capturing certain phrases or transition statements or counting the number of times a person's name is used. Observation goes beyond facts and can include drawing inferences or forming a judgment about something. At the heart of observation, though, is being aware of a person or situation for the purpose of consciously thinking about what you observe relative to the outcome or behavior of others—with the express purpose of influencing your own behavior. Observation often makes us want to replicate behavior or, conversely, to avoid certain behaviors.

Social Modeling

Albert Bandura, a prominent psychologist, put forth social learning theory, which essentially suggests that people learn from one another and do so via observation, imitation, and ultimately behavioral modeling.[1] Social modeling, also known as social learning, posits that we learn and change behavior by watching the actions of others. That is, what is learned is learned in and through the environment. When you watch and observe people, they essentially become a model whether it is their intent or not. Bandura stated that there are four "mediational processes" that influence social learning: attention, retention, reproduction, and motivation.[2] When behavior modeling is done for the purpose of learning or training, it takes on certain characteristics. In apprenticeships, for example, the apprentice observes, learns, and gains skills from watching a master perform a task or series of specialized tasks. Although apprenticeships are not common in most U.S. workplaces, the concept of behavior modeling as a learning tool is quite common—and useful.

For effective learning to take place, Bandura said that these four conditions are necessary. In addition, there is a strong and reciprocal relationship between the person and his or her environment with respect to the person's behavior. The first condition, *attention*, assumes that a variety of factors both in the environment and in the individual affect attention. These factors can either increase or decrease the amount of attention one pays. An environment that is unique, not previously experienced, or complex could direct the attention of some individuals to cues or information others may not see. Individuals with greater sensory capacity or a different perceptual orientation may discern and attend to details not noticed by someone else. For example, some supervisors may notice if an employee is having an off day, and others may not.

The second condition, *retention*, has to do with what you remember and how you remember what you paid attention to in the environment. Whether we realize it or not, we all code what we see in some fashion—we do this with both verbal and nonverbal information. We may code an item as important or unimportant, positive, or possibly alarming. We may retain certain images, and we may organize what we observed in some fashion. But the key for behavioral modeling is that you retain the information or behavior so you can reproduce it. As an HR director, you may want to improve your skill and comfort level in building relationships with board members in dealing with the compensation committee. As a result, you might focus on watching your immediate supervisor or the head of the company to see how each engages board members and how the meeting unfolds with respect to following the stated agenda.

Reproduction, the third condition or stage, refers to how well, if at all, you can *reproduce* the model's actions. It's one thing to watch your boss "work the room" and run an effective committee meeting and another to replicate the same results when you are in the position to have to do this on your own. Reproduction does not imply that you must do everything exactly the same or that you retain exact details. The idea behind modeling is that you are trying to influence your own behavior and performance. Observers may not yet have the skills or ability to reproduce the actions they would like to emulate. But observation can provide ideas and actions to mirror as well as insight into the behaviors one needs to practice and develop to imitate those ideas and actions.

Motivation, the final condition, has to do with individuals having a good reason to want to reproduce the effective behaviors they've seen. What, if any, stimulus exists that provides the impetus to want to change behavior? We all have different motives or influences that give us the reasons why we might want to change our behavior. Paying attention, retaining, and even reproducing will be influenced greatly by how motivated we are to develop ourselves. We may or may not think our behavior needs to change, and we may or may not want to follow through and make those changes.

This chapter does not suggest that behavioral modeling per se be followed. However, it is suggested that considering how social learning takes place can be a beneficial approach to developing your HR behavioral competencies. Purposeful observation can help you reflect on your own behavior relative to others to understand what might be effective and ineffective behavior in the performance of your role as an HR professional.

Overt versus Covert Observation

Observation can be either covert or overt. When you observe others in an overt way, you usually tell them that you are observing them and why you are doing so. If you make your purpose known, you can then initiate follow-up conversations with the people being observed to better understand their behavior and their competence in a situation. For example, you might want to ask your supervisor about attending the compensation committee meeting of the board so that you can see what is done and gain business acumen for the future. On the other hand, when people know they are being observed, they may or may not act naturally, and this may or may not reveal their true behavior. As the observer, you can decide how much to disclose about your efforts. Being open is most often a good practice, but the dynamics of your scenario may lead you to think otherwise. In addition, being able to observe unplanned interesting interactions is something to capitalize on.

When observation is done covertly, the observer can watch from a distance or even be part of the situation being observed—the compensation committee meeting for example. Covert observation occurs all the time and does not imply that we are "spies." When done purposefully, covert observation implies that there is intent behind our actions. An advantage to the observer in this situation is that the people being observed will act naturally. By contrast, in the case of the compensation committee, being observed may influence not just your supervisor but the board members as well. Although the board members may not know that an observer is there for a specific reason, an additional person in the room can change the dynamic. This is what Bandura meant by reciprocal interaction. Another advantage to observing covertly is that if you observe people with the express purpose of learning, you do not need to obtain their permission to do so. To be fair, it is true that we observe people every day—both overtly and covertly. However, the suggestion in this chapter is that, to strengthen the advantages of observation, we should be more disciplined and goal-oriented and that, therefore, observation should be conducted in a more dedicated manner. It is sometimes difficult to distinguish between overt and covert observation since the primary difference is whether or not you let the target know that he or she is being observed for a purpose. Regardless, both overt and covert observations are relatively easy to do, and few resources are needed by the observer to carry out a meaningful exercise. However easy they may be, though, the observer must be careful not to be distracting—especially if he or she is part of the scenario (for example, a meeting). A final advantage is that both kinds of observations can be done over time—making the analysis longitudinal and allowing the observer to interpret behavioral differences in both situations and in the individual, based on his or her growth.

To make your observation a more effective learning tool, add some structure to it. Structure need not be cumbersome or detailed but may provide context to add meaning and easier interpretation of the behaviors observed. Although observation can be overt, the reality is that it will most often be covert. You may or may not enter a situation with the purpose of observing and recording observations. More often, you may simply find yourself carefully observing and taking notes, which lead to your own education and learning. Allowing yourself the luxury of gaining wisdom through observation may give you ideas about how to adjust your own behavior. By observing the whole situation, you may derive guidance that you had not thought of previously. For example, you may be prompted to take a class or seek a mentor. Caution must be exercised, though, because one observation may be interesting and thought-provoking, but it may not be indicative of a pattern or a behavior likely to work or be replicated. Before you make final interpretations or judgments, observe behavior over time to ensure it works, or engage in further discussion about what you noticed.

Coaching Tip

As an HR leader, you can prompt your staff to be observant and to recognize that there are learning moments to be gained throughout observation. If you recognize something interesting or significant in a meeting or interaction, ask your staff or colleagues if they witnessed the same thing—ask what people noticed, what they thought it meant, and how it might influence their own behavior. The discussion alone about the observation can provide learning and insight.

Putting Structure into Observation

As an observer, you may have some choices to make with respect to your approach. For example, you can decide in advance that certain behaviors or events will be noted and that other behaviors will be ignored. Decide what you will pay attention to and what you proactively want to remember. For example, you may decide to observe an executive in a particular setting and to pay special attention to certain behaviors. You may decide, for instance, to observe the senior most HR professional in your organization during weekly staff meetings to see how he or she solicits ideas or input from others. There will likely be a lot going on in the weekly meeting, but if you confine your observation to a single theme, you may be able to garner more specific information about a competency and not just a single behavior. By homing in on a single behavior or concept, you may be able to gain specific insights and see patterns that you had not previously noticed. Observations such as these can be replicated, and the focus of the observation can be changed once you have generated ideas and inferences.

To aid in the usefulness of observation, you may want to devise a chart to help gather data. The chart can be more formal, such as the one in Worksheet 8.1, or it can be less formal and consist simply of notes that you keep on a physical notepad or an electronic device. Record enough information to ensure that the observation is useful to you.

Specific Behaviors of a Specific Target or Model

Decide in advance who your target is and what behaviors or competencies you plan to observe. Be as specific as possible. Start narrow—you can always expand the parameters of your observation. For example, if observing your supervisor run a staff meeting, you can start by focusing on one small aspect and then expand as time goes on.

Specific Target to Observe

Select someone whose behaviors and actions can provide an insightful learning opportunity. You can select a boss, another executive, a peer, or even a subordinate. Everyone has different strengths, and almost everyone can provide fodder for learning—even if the orientation is on what *not* to do in a given situation. After some initial focus on your supervisor in a staff meeting, you may want to focus on a peer who is displaying challenging (or effective) behaviors.

WORKSHEET 8.1 PLAN AN OBSERVATION

Instructions: Be sure to include the date(s) of the event and to describe the event(s) to provide context for the learning.

Date	Event
Behavior(s)	
Target	
Recipient's reaction	
Outcome(s)	
Your own reactions	
Target adjustment	
Motivation	

Recipient Reaction to the Target or Behaviors Observed

Not only are observing and recording the behavior of your target meaningful, but also critical is how the recipient or recipients of the behavior react to what has been said or done. Recipient reactions may or may not be immediate. Reactions may or may not be verbal. If you observe something you think is effective—make sure that you have evidence that this reaction is shared by others. If it is not— try to explore what the difference is and why. Understanding your perceptions relative to others' perceptions can be quite enlightening.

Outcomes That Occur Based on the Behaviors

Some outcomes may be readily apparent, while others may take time to occur or may not be as easily discernible. If you are specific enough in what you are observing, looking for outcomes or charting what has occurred as a result may be easier.

Your Own Reaction to What You've Observed

What was your own response to the behavior you witnessed? Did it seem effective or ineffective to you, and why? Did you feel that it was something you could emulate in a way that would be comfortable and natural? How did you think others would react, and did their immediate or later reactions align with your thinking?

Target Reactions to the Reaction of Others

If the behavior of the target that you have chosen to observe causes others to react to the target, how did the target react to the reactions? For example, if you are observing how a manager dismisses comments of certain group members and this behavior results in negative behavior from others in the group, how did the manager react to the negative behavior of others in the situation? Did the target modify his or her behavior in the scenario to account for reactions or outcomes of others (recipients) in the situation?

Motivation

What is your motivation to observe a particular behavior or target? How might this motivation influence what you do or don't do with what you learned from your surveillance? You may also want to think about what the motivations were behind what you observed. This may help in thinking through what you observed. There are two motivations at issue here. One is *your* motivation to observe something, and the other is a perception about what the motivation was behind the behavior you observed and from the person you observed. Your motivation and *their* motivation.

Capturing Your Observations

The points above can be captured in a worksheet such as the one provided—in Worksheet 8.1 and the sample provided in the Appendix, or they can be captured in a journal. In fact, you can use a journal for several days or weeks or on a regular basis to help you identify the behaviors, situations, or targets that you want to observe more formally. Observation can help highlight communication or other "techniques" that may be useful for you. From this standpoint, being as disciplined and as concrete in your approach as possible is advised. Keeping a competency journal can be an effective habit to develop.

Competency Journal

Journaling is a popular and effective tool for capturing your experiences and learning moments. Many lessons can be learned from everyday life—both at work and outside of work. The lessons can be great illustrations of what to do more of—or less of if behavior has not been effective. Sometimes while we are focused on doing things, we may miss some powerful learning or wisdom by observing actions or behaviors that may serve us well in other contexts.

By keeping a competency journal, you will be actively reflecting on your experience. Recording your thoughts can shed light on useful insights about how you demonstrated your competencies. These insights can provide you with valuable understanding and interpretation for the future and also help you develop your own personalized feedback system. How you construct your competency journal is completely up to you. It can be written in a journal or kept as a running file on a mobile phone or tablet. Regardless of where you capture your insights, the following general approaches will help you stay organized and allow you to get the most out of your effort:

- *Capture the event.* There will typically be an event, exchange, or activity that prompts you to consider making a journal entry. It can be anything you experience—at work or elsewhere. The objective in journaling is to depict the scenario as accurately and as objectively as possible. This can be challenging especially if you have difficulty either praising yourself or criticizing yourself. The more detailed you can make your entries, the better:

  - Not detailed: John, the manager of our IT group, was not receptive to my coaching.
  - Detailed: I saw John, the manager of our IT group, in the parking lot and provided him with some feedback about his style to help him. He was rude and not receptive to my feedback.

  Rereading your journal entry a week later will be clearer with the greater detail—and it may lead you to see a pattern or make a pivotal insight.

- Identify your reaction. Capture how you behaved in the situation. Identify your actions, words, and thoughts or feelings at the time. You may want to record noticeable or salient responses from you or others in the scenario as you reflect on the event. For example, in the case of John, the IT manager, you might identify what you wanted to do versus what you did, and what you thought or how you felt. Did you walk away rather than say something (about Joe's rudeness)? Did you frown or tell him his behavior was inappropriate? Did you think there was something you could or should have done differently? Here are some questions to consider for your journal entries:

  - *What did you actually do?*
    Frowned, smile, shook my head
    Asked . . .
    Told/said . . .
  - *What did you want to do in that moment?*
    I wanted to say/argue that . . .
    I wanted to walk away . . .
  - *What were you feeling?*
    Anxious/angry/sad that I felt misunderstood
    Positive about the exchange
    That he or she didn't know me
  - *What did you think?*
    Well, that's John
    Why does this always happen to me?
    Boy, I really blew it.

- *Pinpoint your learning.* After identifying the event and what you were thinking and feeling, you need to pinpoint your learning and which competencies you think should be highlighted as examples of effective behavior and those that present an opportunity for learning and development. For example, you ponder the following:

  ‹ What does the event, exchange, or activity and my reactions to it tell me about my own *communication* competency and the issues on which I might need to work?

  ‹ Are there signs that I am progressing in my *leadership* and *navigation* or that I need more practice?

  ‹ Is there a pattern here that I haven't seen with respect to my ability in *relationship management*?

  ‹ Is there something to be learned from this scenario that might help me with my consultation skills or that will help me understand what needs to be done with respect to *critical evaluation*?

  ‹ What might I do in the future that will help me regarding *global and cultural awareness*?

Your learning can focus on just one or two competencies or on more. The aim, however, is to identify a learning that will help you improve or help you think about how you might apply what you learned in a different setting. You may or may not have immediate answers to the questions you raise. In addition, your learning may evolve as you encounter the same person or similar scenario in subsequent interactions. This is one of the advantages of keeping a competency journal. You can detect patterns and see how your own behaviors evolve over time. Worksheet 8.2, along with a completed example in the Appendix, may provide some guidance as to how to approach your observational efforts.

Observation Differences by Level

Observation is a ubiquitous activity, and because it can be done either actively or passively, it is applicable to all levels of HR professionals. During your early career, the *entry-level* HR professional should focus first and foremost on observing others in the HR profession and secondarily on others in the organization and business community. Observing other HR professionals will not only help you develop needed behaviors; it will also help you think about on which specialty areas of HR you may want to focus, or more broadly, which industries or sectors are more appealing as a good fit.

WORKSHEET 8.2 OBSERVATION DATA COLLECTION WORKSHEET	
Target of observation (who/what):	
Observation scenario:	
Behaviors noted:	Comments:
Overall Observations and Key Takeaways:	

Instructions: Select a focus for your observation. It could be a person or an event. Be narrow enough that you can find meaningful facts/information to note. Be specific in the behaviors you note and in your comments as to whether the behavior is effective or ineffective; note any follow-up questions.

As you move forward in your HR career, observing others in business both inside and outside HR, or inside or outside your organization, can help broaden your perspective. At both the *mid level* and *senior level*, though, your observation should be much more structured to help you capture the most insights. At these levels you will have far more access than at the entry level to a variety of meetings and professional scenarios. Take advantage of these opportunities for more structured observation, and think of ways you can create opportunities for observation that will be advantageous to you. As you learn from your observations, you may then want to spend more time thinking about the motivations behind observations to aid in your own ability to coach and develop others.

By the time you reach the *executive level* of your career, your powers of observation will likely be far more honed than at any previous level. In addition to observing those around you for developmental insights or new perspectives, you may also want to structure your observation to help others in your HR organization or other peers in different functions. When you observe others with the objective of providing them with feedback or insights about their behaviors or the behaviors of others relative to them, your observation takes on a different orientation and can actually be developmental from a different perspective. You will use a different skill set when your observation is done to assist others rather than just yourself. Don't shy away from expressing your observations for the purpose of helping others with their own competency development.

Chapter Summary

- Purposeful observation offers an opportunity to learn and absorb through consciously noticing one's surroundings and interactions.
- Social modeling, in concept, can provide a framework that will help you understand how observation can be used to develop HR competencies.
- Observation is done all the time, and putting structure into the process can enrich the learning experience.
- Keeping a competency journal to capture your observations of others relative to HR competencies can help you sort and categorize effective and ineffective behaviors.

Additional Resources for Purposeful Observation

Bingham, T., and Conner, M. *The New Social Learning*, 2nd ed. San Francisco: Association for Talent Development and Berrett-Koehler, 2015.

Hoover, D., Giambatista, R., and Belkin, L. "Eyes On, Hands On: Vicarious Observational Learning as an Enhancement of Direct Experience." *Academy of Management Learning and Education Journal* 11, no. 4 (2012): 591-608.

Klosowski, T. (2015). "How to Boost Your Observation Skills and Learn to Pay Attention." http://lifehacker.com/how-to-boost-your-observation-skills-and-learn-to-pay-a-1678229721.

Morris, C. "Teaching and Learning through Active Observation." 2014. https://

www.researchgate.net/publication/252762848_Teaching_and_learning_through_active_observation.

Rosenthal, T., and Zimmerman, B. *Social Learning and Cognition*. New York: Academic Press, 1978.

CHAPTER 9

Volunteering

Benefits of Volunteering for HR Competency Development

Volunteering to help others either inside your organization or in the external environment can provide many opportunities and benefits for HR competency development:

- Offering an alternative way to receive training in a particular area.
- Allowing you to test new areas in which you may be interested or in which you may have knowledge, skills, abilities, and other characteristics (KSAOs).
- Allowing for nonthreatening examination of potentially different career avenues.
- Providing professional development; the fee is your time rather than your dollars. You can learn something new, or get better at something you already do.
- Furnishing a typically low risk opportunity with little chance of being "let go."
- Providing an excellent opportunity for additional observation, discussion, and networking.
- Building skills and strength and behaviors that will make you more valuable on the job or in your next career pursuits.
- Exposing you to experiences you may not be able to gain at work.
- Building confidence and courage.
- Developing coaching and mentoring skills.

Volunteering is generally considered an altruistic activity in which an individual or group provides services for no financial gain. It is often motivated by altruistic intentions or to the desire to improve an individual's quality of life. Also well known for skill development, volunteering may have positive benefits for the volunteer as well as for the person or group served. It may also be less altruistic and intended to make contacts for possible employment or for personal and professional gain. The intangible benefits of volunteering—such as pride, satisfaction, and accomplishment—are worthwhile reasons to serve. Tangible benefits of learning a new skill, gaining experience, and expanding your circle of acquaintances are also worthwhile.

Volunteering is much more than a networking activity, although it certainly has that quality. Volunteering can provide you with an opportunity to build, practice, and develop your skills, abilities, and behaviors in an environment that can be safe and even nurturing. If you want to volunteer outside of your organization and for a cause that is important to you, make sure the situation provides you with the benefits of practice and safety. Capitalize on this. Have an open mind and ask to do more or different things than what you're already good at—of course you may be asked to volunteer your known strength, but try to stretch and go beyond this in a meaningful way. Take the opportunity to ask questions and learn as much as possible.

In this chapter we will consider two different approaches to volunteering. The first is when you volunteer as part of your job or as part of your role as an HR professional and includes actions like mentoring, coaching, or taking on additional assignments outside your normal role. The second approach is when you volunteer in a charitable or professional organization. In this setting you are outside your typical confines. If volunteering inside your organization, some of the benefits identified at the start of the chapter may be diminished in that there is more risk and the potential to influence your current role. For example, your supervisor or others in the organization may evaluate your extra activity without separating the behaviors from your regular role. It may be difficult for others in the organization to distinguish what you intend as a learning experience from your "performance" in the organization. However, since the upside may also be greater, effort should be made to clarify and distinguish the activity as a voluntary effort to develop your skills.

A more formal definition of volunteering is "giving time or skills during a planned activity for a volunteer group or organization."[1] One key point in this definition is that the giving is active (giving of personal time and effort) rather than passive (such as in giving money). A second point is that the activity is planned rather than spontaneous. And the final point is that it occurs in a particular context—that of a volunteer or charitable organization. In applying the notion of volunteering to developing one's behavioral competencies, we can extend the final point to also include one's existing organization—which may or may not be a charitable organization.

Research into volunteering has been sparse, but some common themes have emerged. One area of investigation has looked at why people volunteer.[2] The motivations behind volunteering have been characterized as either intrinsic or extrinsic. Given that volunteering is an unpaid activity and often outside the confines of one's job, the motivation for volunteering needs to come from someplace. Those who are intrinsically motivated may do so because of the inherent value they derive from helping someone or something or because they enjoy the activity itself. Extrinsic factors, on the other hand, come from outside the individual and include outward factors that compel someone to be motivated to volunteer—social norms, for example.

HR professionals who are motivated to build and develop their behavioral competencies may be both intrinsically and extrinsically motivated. Therefore, applying the concept of volunteering to develop one's competencies makes practical sense and provides another opportunity for development. Moreover, it includes the added benefit of helping someone or some organization in addition to one's self. We know from existing research that the meaningfulness of volunteer activities can in and of itself drive volunteering. Research also suggests that if paid jobs are less meaningful, employees may be more likely to increase or seek volunteering activities to enhance or gain their desired sense of meaning.[3] If volunteering compensates for jobs or positions that do not provide meaning, then it may also hold true that volunteering for the purpose of enhancing one's experience and skill makes sense.

If your professional role within your organization provides exposure only to certain activities or experiences and your desire is to advance either inside or outside your organization, then you will need to develop your skills and abilities elsewhere. Behavioral competencies by definition can't be learned by just reading or hearing about them—you must actually practice doing them. Furthermore, since there are at least four levels of proficiency related to career levels, even if you have the opportunity to build your skills in a certain competency area, it may not take you as far as you need to go. For example, if your organization is relatively small or your role is at a mid level with limited opportunity to go beyond this, it may be difficult to build up your behaviors in leadership and navigation, relationship management, ethical practice, or any of the other behavioral competencies at a higher level of performance. Consider the following possibilities for volunteering.

Volunteer to Mentor Someone

Consider mentoring someone in a different discipline than HR. For example, if you become a mentor to someone in finance, you will, through discussions and over time, learn about the stressors or key aspects of what a finance professional does. You won't become an expert in finance, but you will expand your own perspective—while helping someone else. Developing leadership and navigation behaviors means that you understand all parts of the organization and that you can influence others. Becoming a mentor and helping guide someone else will not only help the protégé; it will also have the added benefit of developing yourself. Mentoring is not about power—it is or can be mutually beneficial and should not be based on power differences. Instruction in the situation is not based on pressure to behave in a certain way—it is fundamentally about teaching. Being aware that mentoring someone else can also be highly developmental is one way to derive benefit from something you may already do.

Volunteer to Coach a Peer Who Works Inside *or* Outside the HR Discipline

Coaching is more directive than mentoring. And while coaching may be inherent in a job in which you are a people manager, coaching could extend to outside your immediate span of control. For example, if you see a colleague who consistently fails to get his or her point across or who has difficulty speaking in front of a group, you can build your own skill while helping the person develop his or her skill and performance. As a coach, your role is to be impartial, and the purpose is to focus on improving someone's behavior. Putting yourself in this role will help you develop your skills in observation, analytics, relationship management, and much more.

Volunteering in the examples above is often a matter of choice and is not required of the giver. The point of these examples is to identify opportunities that may take you out of your comfort zone or out of a situation that offers limited opportunities for development. And while mentoring or coaching may to some degree be a part of your existing role, extending your efforts beyond your role or your organization by volunteering can be beneficial.

Coaching Tip

It may not occur to entry- or midcareer professionals to volunteer to mentor or coach. But with direction from an HR leader, these individuals may be able to form a mutually beneficial relationship by volunteering to partner with others at the same or more junior level.

Tips for Seeking Volunteer Activities

Volunteering for the purpose of professional development may not come as easily as volunteering to help at a school charity function, which is a fairly defined volunteer activity. Look at volunteering for development with a different lens.

- *Research.* Investigate an opportunity when it arises, or research the causes or issues that are most important to you and that might offer you the best opportunity to develop a particular competency.

- *Consider what you have to offer.* Look for a volunteer opportunity in which your knowledge, skills, and abilities can be used. Finding ways to contribute may lead to greater opportunities for you to learn. Think about your personality and how your abilities and behaviors might fit with different organizations or activities.

- *Think outside the box.* Whether inside or outside your organization, you can look to volunteer in a completely different role.

- *Don't wait to be asked.* There are many ways to find others in your organization or in outside organizations who are looking for volunteers. Ask your friends or colleagues about their own volunteering activities.

- *Be proactive.* When you find an opportunity that is in line with your interests, plan for your meeting with your possible volunteer manager in much the same way that you would plan for a job interview. Be ready to describe your interests, qualifications, and background, and also be prepared to ask your interviewers about the opportunity and the benefits the organization offers their volunteers. An interview will allow you and the organization to find the right match for your skills and interests. Don't be afraid to create an opportunity where none specifically exists.

- *Learn something new.* Consider whether the organization offers training or professional development opportunities for its volunteers. Or, if training is not provided, is there an orientation or some mechanism to get to know the organization and its business objectives? Volunteering can provide you with the chance to learn about something you're interested in and develop skills in a new area and can provide an opportunity to learn about a new or different organization.

- *Find the volunteer activity that fits your schedule.* Organizations need different levels of commitment for different types of volunteer activities. Serving as a mentor, for example, requires a regular, potentially intensive commitment, while volunteering to talk to a student who may be interested in the profession may be a one-time commitment.

- *Volunteer with friends or family.* Think about looking for a volunteer opportunity that would be suitable for parents and children to do together, or for spouse or a group of friends to take on as a team. This might provide you with a different perspective that can be instrumental in learning something new. Volunteering with others can be a great way to get to know them better and can help keep you excited about volunteering. And it can be a beneficial way to receive feedback on your own behaviors.

- *Stretch yourself.* If you're looking to expose yourself to activities that you have little opportunity to do in your current role, do not shy away from an experience that may provide you with this chance—even if you've never done the activity previously. The stretch should not be too great as this will cause excessive stress and may increase the likelihood of failure. But a little stretch will provide you with the motivation and focus to be successful.

Table 9.1 provides some specific examples of volunteer activities to consider, broken down by behavioral competencies. The activities in the table are suggestions of how you can initiate volunteer activities that might be tailored to your personal development needs. For example, if you need to develop business acumen and you believe you have limited opportunities in your current role, think through what will help you develop, and then propose or create this activity—if one does not already exist. The suggestions in this table can help you search for the opportunities or create them.

As you consider volunteering as a way to help others and yourself, keep in mind the eight HR behavioral competencies and try to match the outcomes sought with your HR competency needs. For HR professionals, a wonderful opportunity exists within the HR profession itself. The Society for Human Resource Management, for example, has a network in the U.S. of over 575 professional chapters and more than 250 student chapters across the country.

TABLE 9.1 SUGGESTIONS FOR VOLUNTEER ACTIVITIES

Business Acumen	• Volunteer to conduct an environmental scan for your local business environment or in a market into which the organization is hoping to explore. • Volunteer to help at a local business school and immerse yourself in a wide range of activities (outside of HR).
Communication	• Volunteer to administer a survey for your local SHRM chapter, and then develop communications for the board, the members, and the public about the results. • Become the communications officer at a local professional organization such as the Chamber of Commerce.
Consultation	• Offer your KSAOs as a volunteer to a local charity or nonprofit organization. • Volunteer to identify change management strategies that might be necessary in another business unit of your organization or in a local charity.
Critical Evaluation	• Look for an opportunity to help an organization build the evidence it needs for a new initiative. • Volunteer to help a colleague evaluate and analyze a new business opportunity currently out of your scope.
Ethical Practice	• Volunteer to give a speech about ethical practice to a local organization such as the Chamber of Commerce. • Volunteer to be the ethics officer for your local SHRM chapter or at the state council level.
Global and Cultural Effectiveness	• Help a local charitable organization or nonprofit with understanding diversity and inclusion—apply what you know to a new or different situation. • Develop a cultural awareness program within your organization for another business unit.
Leadership and Navigation	• Volunteer to help articulate the goals, vision, or strategy for a local professional or charitable organization. • Volunteer to be a leader or take on a more substantive role in a local SHRM chapter or in the state council.
Relationship Management	• Volunteer to be a liaison of some sort in a local organization, such as the Chamber or local business network, or create a business network. • Volunteer to be the communications officer for a local SHRM organization.

Then there are some 35 networks across the world as well. These groups are all volunteer managed. Many opportunities exist to get involved in these groups and to help yourself while helping other local HR professionals. This type of volunteering does require a commitment, but there are a variety of roles—some more formal or extensive than others.

Other volunteer activities to consider include:

- Charity organization—locally or nationally
- Religious organizations or related religious charities
- Local universities or continuing education entities
- Political campaigns
- Local professional HR association or business association
- Local Chamber of Commerce
- Community or civic organization
- Local sports organization

Volunteering has no specific boundaries. Consider any possibility that interests you or which may present itself to you.

Volunteer Differences by Level

Volunteering is something that many of us do throughout our lifetime—often beginning as a teenager. Sometimes it is referred to as community service, and sometimes it is a requirement of school or a religious program. The (positive) consequence is that the concept of volunteering is ingrained in almost all of us. Some may volunteer more than others, and some may volunteer more or less at various life or career stages. Some may volunteer in primarily professional organizations and others for more charitable causes—and others, still, in the combination of the two.

At the *entry level* of your career, which could include your formal education years, volunteering is a good idea for a variety of reasons. You will not only expose yourself to opportunities for development that you may not yet have access to in school or in an early job, but you will also be expanding your network and exploring possible career interest areas. Keep in mind that early-career professionals do not always contribute as much as a more experienced professional when volunteering, but they do bring energy and commitment. At this stage, they may derive as much, if not more, benefit than they give in exchange. Volunteering can be as much about exploring as it is about giving to the community.

At the *mid level*, volunteering can still be developmental in terms of exploring and networking, but at this level you have more to contribute in terms of drawing on your HR expertise and experience. At this level and at the *senior level*, you are more likely to be able to secure substantive volunteer roles and roles that may take you closer to relevant HR volunteer opportunities. Volunteering in your local or state SHRM chapter or at a local business (a start-up, for example) or the Chamber of Commerce may provide an excellent source of developmental opportunities, while at the same time building your confidence and skills. Your mid- and senior-level career stages can span a range of years. As a result, you may engage in many different types of volunteering and encounter a variety of settings. Maintaining commitment to one or two preferred organizations is certainly fine, but keep in mind that from a developmental perspective, looking for assignments and roles that will be successively more challenging or different will provide you with more opportunity for developing your HR competencies.

At the *executive level*, volunteering can take on many different faces and provide a wealth of new experiences that are valuable both to you and to the organizations for which you volunteer. For example, you may be invited to sit on a council, board, taskforce, or committee for assignments that are at the national or international level. You may be sought out because of your reputation, and you may reach for these assignments and be selected due to your expertise. The roles may likely be at a leadership level and provide you an opportunity to meet people outside your typical circles or organization.

Chapter Summary

- Networking, skill building, and exposure to areas outside your current job or personal domain can be gained through volunteering.
- Opportunity to test or experiment with activities to determine if you like them and would like to develop the associated behaviors are available through volunteering.
- Volunteering offers a chance to help others while helping yourself.
- Opportunities abound and can be tailored to your time and availability.

Additional Resources for Volunteering

Geisler, C., Okum, M., and Grano, C. "Who Is Motivated to Volunteer? A Latent Profile Analysis Linking Volunteer Motivation to Frequency of Volunteering." *Psychological Test and Assessment Modeling* 56, no. 1 (2014): 3-24.

Hoseo, M. "Six leadership Skills You Can Gain from Volunteering." *Marketing Week*. July 2, 2015. https://www.marketingweek.com/2015/07/02/six-leadership-skills-you-can-gain-from-volunteering/.

Patel, N. "Develop Leadership Skills through Volunteering." 2014. http://ewh.ieee.org/r1/new_hampshire//Docs/2010-08-NP1.pdf.

Rink, T., Sarola, A., and Vargha, R. (2015). "Volunteering 101: What's in It for You?" *Information Outlook* 18, no. 5 (September/October 2014): 22-29.

Rodell, J. B. "Finding Meaning through Volunteering: Why Do Employees Volunteer and What Does It Mean for Their Jobs?" *Academy of Management Journal* 56, no. 5 (2013): 1274-1294.

Tharp, J. Volunteering Value. *PM Network*. December 2015, 3-5.

Portfolio

Benefits of Creating a Portfolio for HR Competency Development

Creating a file of career- and competency-related data creates a nice archive and can also provide a number of additional benefits for competency development:

- Achieving flexibility; portfolios have multiple uses for development.
- Helping to promote achievements when used as an effective marketing tool if looking for a job or promotion.
- Providing a great way to organize and showcase accomplishments.
- Creating an archive for easy access to and protection for all your career-related documents.
- Creating a personal database that is portable.
- Demonstrating your professionalism and organization.
- Providing a roadmap and signal of where your gaps may exist.
- Highlighting your potential.
- Creating dual-purpose portfolios: a learning portfolio and a job portfolio.

A portfolio is a tangible collection of items that demonstrate what you know *and* what you're able to do. A portfolio can be useful to any HR professional to help identify the significant things you've accomplished and above all, where and how you've developed your competencies. Additionally, a portfolio can help identify where you have both gaps and strengths. A portfolio is like a personalized briefcase that helps you organize your career accomplishments, your aspirations, and your developmental needs.

From a practical perspective, a portfolio can be a physical file or notebook or can be kept as an electronic file. A portfolio can be for your own personal use or can be used to help you showcase your abilities in the search for a new opportunity. Once created, a portfolio should be maintained and kept up-to-date. A portfolio does not take the place of a resume but certainly can be used to supplement one. And a portfolio is not a development plan per se but certainly can complement and provide direction for a development plan.

How to Use a Portfolio

As an HR professional, you can organize your portfolio in a variety of ways. Organizing a portfolio around HR behavioral competencies makes the most sense for developmental purposes. Organizing around career highlights or jobs may also make sense if your primary objective is job advancement irrespective of any development goals you may have. Much of the work and activities that an HR professional does can be captured in a variety of ways. For example, many activities in employee relations involve competencies such as communication, relationship management, ethical practice, critical evaluation, and so forth. If you took the results of an engagement survey and ran an analysis that compared business units and drew conclusions on which the organization could make process or policy decisions, this might be something to include as a discrete demonstration of critical evaluation. The following summarizes how a portfolio might be used:

- Prepare for an interview.
- Create a development plan.
- Track progress in developing competencies.
- Have a development discussion with a boss or peer.
- Keep track of professional development.
- Highlight accomplishments during a performance review.
- Demonstrate your professionalism.
- Market your accomplishments.

Not everything you do (for example, reports, analyses) should be put in a portfolio. But if the document represents a significant undertaking, is something you're proud of, or is representative of something unique that you've never done before, then it should be given consideration for inclusion in the portfolio. Below are some examples and ideas to consider.

Things to Include in a Portfolio

- An up-to-date table of contents.
- Key report, written by you, that demonstrates strategic thinking, excellent writing, or innovation.
- A presentation (for example, PowerPoint, Prezi, or Google Slides) you've done that demonstrates strategic thinking and a clear presentation of ideas.
- A chart or diagram that is creative and impressive for its clarity and high-level thinking.
- An analysis you completed that demonstrates critical thinking or highlights another competency in the SHRM Competency Model.
- Certification(s) or certificates that demonstrate continuous learning.
- Articles about you from local, national, or company publications.
- Awards that you've received.
- Articles, books, or book chapters that you've written.
- Presentations you've been invited to make to outside groups—outside the normal course of your job.
- Grants or proposals that you've written and which have been funded or approved.
- Anything that demonstrates what you've done or showcases your knowledge, skills, abilities, and other characteristics (KSAOs).
- Thank-you notes or notes of congratulations.
- Details about significant volunteer activities.
- Reports to which you contributed even if you were not the sole author.
- Teams or committees on which you served; you may also want to include sports teams or other extracurricular team activities.
- Leadership roles you've held both inside and outside the organization.
- Educational or professional development accomplishments, including copies of your diplomas, licensures, and relevant certifications.

- Assessment results such as tests or diagnostic tools (for example, Myers-Brigg Type Indicator).

- Specialty training, such as military training, you have completed; it is generally a good idea to keep a running list or spreadsheet with relevant dates, credits and other information of the training, seminars, conferences, or workshops you've attended.

- Resume—one, or the evolution of your resume over a span of time.

- Letters of reference you have received over the years for job searches or award applications.

- Work samples—for example, policies or surveys.

- Grade or transcript reports as appropriate.

- References—you may want to keep a list of people you have used for references or whom you think you could approach for references.

Coaching Tip

An HR career may span many decades. All too often we may find ourselves saying or thinking about something we did in the early part of our career that was pivotal—but for which we only have a memory and nothing more tangible. Remind your staff and others about the value of keeping items like those mentioned above. The value that can be derived in terms of charting development and planning for further development is immense. Keep in mind that you can coach your peers (inside and outside your organization) on these points as well.

Being organized with your portfolio is essential if the portfolio is to serve as a learning activity for HR competency development. See Worksheet 10.1 for a template of how you might organize your portfolio. This chart can be used to identify developmental needs. See the sample portfolio in Table 10.1 that is focused on the leadership and navigation competency. Accessibility and usability will be key to getting the most out of your portfolio. Now consider the following characteristics of a portfolio to help you interpret your own portfolio and maintain its usefulness.

WORKSHEET 10.1 PORTFOLIO PLANNING WORKSHEET

Competency	Items that could fit in Portfolio	Do you have this item?			
		YES		NO	
		✓	Date Attained	✓	How to Attain
EXAMPLE — Communication	• Open enrollment brochure	✓	10/13		
	• Expatriate policy			✓	volunteer
	• Board compensation committee presentation	✓	7/14		
Business Acumen					
Communication					
Consultation					
Critical Evaluation					
Ethical Practice					
Global and Cultural Effectiveness					
Leadership and Navigation					
Relationship Management					

TABLE 10.1 PORTFOLIO CHECKLIST: LEADERSHIP AND NAVIGATION COMPETENCY EXAMPLE

Subcompetencies that lend themselves to a portfolio exercise: Change Management, Mission Driven, Succession Planning, and Project Management.

Subcompetency	Behavior Demonstrated	Portfolio Item
Succession Planning • In 2013, led initiative in 1,500-person organization	• Fostered collaboration among senior team by demonstrating value of succession planning and gathering input to the process • Identified concerns and potential problem in the organization through discussion and one-on-one interviews • Led the organization through steps to be used for succession planning and proposed a template and process	Succession planning template Succession planning process documents • PowerPoint deck • Interview protocol • Recommendations
Change Management	• No organization-wide change initiative to date. » Need to look for an opportunity	

Project Management	• Spearheaded implementation of employee attitude survey
	  » Put out RFP
	  » Interviewed vendors
	  » Created timeline for implementation
		Employee attitude survey document
		
		Survey results reports for 2015, 2013, and 2011
		
		Note: See evolution of report

Mission Driven		

Actions for further development: Need to develop further *leadership and navigation* through *critical evaluation* skills and abilities; employee attitude survey reports have evolved nicely and are widely distributed and discussed, but I need to show a connection to organizational outcomes such as turnover and other costs. Measures and metrics are something I need to get more comfortable with and better at accomplishing.

Dynamic

A portfolio needs to be dynamic from a competency-development perspective. If you're not keeping your portfolio up-to-date, you run the risk of not exercising your abilities to keep your competencies fresh and honed. This means actively looking at the dates you last added notes in a particular category. The jobs of HR professionals can change focus or emphasis depending on the needs of the business. During this process, make sure that you don't neglect any of your competency areas. In reality you probably "practice" these areas daily without direct or explicit realization, but actively thinking about them can be beneficial from a developmental perspective.

Alterability

Because a portfolio is a collection of documents and will serve you over time, it needs to be something that is easily modified. For example, you may want to create an electronic version of the portfolio or a hybrid in which the worksheets and your narratives are in a physical file or notebook and your career-related documents are stored electronically.

Size

Keep the size of your portfolio manageable, and cull old material as you add new material. You don't need to discard older documentation altogether; you can store it in a portfolio archive. Consider whether you are trying to show an evolution of skills or what's relevant to your current career level or aspiration; for example, you may decide not to include transcripts later in your career. You may want to show an evolution in some areas and not in others.

Organization

Are your documents and accomplishments in chronological order, by competency, by organization in which you worked, or by some combination of all? There is no one best way to organize, but the portfolio needs to be logical and follow a flow that is meaningful to you and that allows you to find what you need, when you need it.

Goals and Objectives

Are your goals clearly stated, and do you have a section that includes your objectives and your career aspirations? Goals and objectives should be well articulated and kept up-to-date. You may wish to include previous goals and objectives and note whether and when they have been accomplished. This will provide you with both a historical record and feedback for the future.

Picture

Do you have a professional portrait? Do you feel comfortable including it? The picture could be for your own use or for external uses. Seeing your own evolution through professional pictures may be reinforcing to you with respect to the path you have taken in your career.

Portability

How portable is your portfolio, and how is it stored? Is it saved on a storage thumb drive or in the cloud, or have you created a website? More importantly, do you have a backup? How accessible is them material if you need to show it to someone in the case of a job search or coaching and mentoring engagement?

Organizing Your Portfolio

With your portfolio planning worksheet, Worksheet 10.1, you have many options. You can use an entire page for each competency if you have related items to include, or you can put multiple competencies on a single worksheet page. This decision may depend on how long you've been working as an HR professional. You should be as detailed as necessary to provide clarity about the item and what it might be showcasing. If you list something, you need to have a corresponding item to support the entry. For example, if you create an open enrollment brochure, make sure you have not only a physical copy of the brochure but also an electronic copy. If you've developed more than one open enrollment brochure over time, you have the opportunity to showcase the evolution and development of your own skills. Be sure to capture examples of your work if you move from one job or organization to another.

The format of your chart is really your choice; your objective should be the driver. The portfolio needs to tell the story of what you've achieved or accomplished, and it needs to have an overarching objective or specific goals that come through. To this end, the portfolio should have a table of contents and include narrative sections—one of which identifies your portfolio goals. For example, if you review your chart and notice that a particular competency does not have many supporting documents, you can set a goal to achieve development that will allow you to collect an appropriate example. Your portfolio is not only an effective marketing tool—it is a way to collect and protect your career-related documents and to identify your gaps.

The portfolio checklist (Table 10.1 above) provides an example of how you might organize your portfolio by subcompetencies that you want to highlight, such as succession planning, change management, project management, or mission-driven activities. Or you can highlight work you may have done given your industry or the size or type of your organization. The breakdowns are really up to you, and it may make sense to see what career-related documents you have before creating your organizing structure.

An additional component of your portfolio is that it should identify gaps or additional goals that you may want to accomplish. For example, if you haven't created a succession plan, but think it would be good for your development to do so, then you should have a to-do list in your portfolio. You may want to prioritize the items on the list or break them down by what is doable in your organization or in your current role. If you are not able to create a succession plan in your current role, either because your organization is too small or not in need of or receptive to a succession plan, then you might brainstorm how to achieve this milestone. For instance, you might look to volunteer to create a plan for an outside organization. Your portfolio is a visual representation of what you've done and the purpose is to highlight your KSAOs. But it can also be designed to showcase your potential. Creating a to-do list of the tangible materials you want to include can show foresight and aspiration.

Portfolio Differences by Level

Portfolios are useful at all levels of one's career. They provide a historical reference of your achievements and create a living roadmap of where you've been and where you may want to go as well as what you may want to accomplish. A portfolio can be focused on both jobs and learning. This chapter suggests that it can be used as self-directed learning device and as an additional way to set career goals. A side benefit of focusing your portfolio on learning is that you are also capturing your accomplishments and therefore can use the portfolio to help you prepare for and document achievements for the purpose of securing another position or different role. To these ends, you may want to also think about the value of your portfolio and how to use it with respect to your HR career level or career aspiration.

At the *entry level*, your portfolio will tend to include educational accomplishments, internships, early-career exploration, and documents that highlight your college major, graduate work, or early performance or acquisition of knowledge and skills. You will not be able to include a long chronology of accomplishments relative to a professional career but focusing on the things you've done to kick-start your career can be helpful. At this stage you may also want to focus on your to-do list of goals to include in your portfolio and how you will go about attaining them. Keep in mind that it may take years to accomplish all that you want to do—look at this as exciting rather than as daunting.

At the *mid level*, you should include more detail about the positions you've held and what you've accomplished. In addition to including examples of your work products or accomplishments, you may also want to demonstrate the logic of your career moves and ask yourself if the progression or positions you've had are in line with what you thought you would be doing or aspire to do. You should create a short bio if you do not already have one. This will be a good benchmark for you as your career progresses. While you may want to deemphasize some of your early activities such as internships, you do want to include much more of a future focus so that your portfolio and your goals have an eye toward aspirations as well as accomplishments.

At the *senior level*, your portfolio will be dependent on your experience, background, and career goals pursued. You may want to begin weeding out more of your earlier career-related documentation in favor of documents that showcase your development—particularly the development of specific HR competencies. For instance, you may want to highlight your leadership, relationship management, ethical practice, and business acumen competencies. Your portfolio may evolve from work samples to highlight team, board, staff, and upper management responsibilities. In addition, since you clearly have accomplished much more and have greater experience, remember to be concise. Include as many documents as you want, but your narratives and other organizing documents should be succinct.

Finally, at the *executive level*, you may want to include an executive resume. Whether you are looking for another position or not, you should always have an up-to-date resume. At this level you are not likely keeping your portfolio to focus specifically on your development needs; rather you may want to highlight a clear summary of accomplishments. Your portfolio can become a teaching tool that you use with junior HR professionals rather than as a roadmap for yourself. The career path that you followed may or may not be right for folks who report to you or who aspire for the top HR job, but it can be illustrative of what can be done and what might be accomplished along the way to support the progression you've enjoyed. Your portfolio should include a bio—both a long one and a short one. At this stage you have likely done enough that your bio will be quite extensive. Additionally, you may want to include some of your professional profiles—such as those you keep on LinkedIn or similar repositories. Lastly, while you likely started to cull items from your portfolio earlier in your career, think about keeping an archive that demonstrates your progression.

Chapter Summary

- A portfolio can be meaningful and useful throughout your entire career.
- A portfolio is a tangible and organized collection of your accomplishments and work samples.
- A portfolio can be focused on both the development side of your career journey as well as the job/position aspirations you may have.
- A portfolio is a way to highlight HR competency development and to focus yourself on any gaps in your competency development that need to be addressed.
- A portfolio is a portable, dynamic development tool.

Additional Resources for Creating an Effective Portfolio

Bozarth, J. *Show Your Work: The Payoffs and How-To's of Working Out Loud.* Hoboken, NJ: Wiley, 2014.

DePaul University Career Center. "Showcase Your Work in an Online Career Portfolio." (n.d.) http://careercenter.depaul.edu/resumes/portfolios.aspx.

Kennedy, J. L. "How an Online Work Portfolio Can Help a Job Search." For

Dummies. (n.d.)
http://www.dummies.com/how-to/content/how-an-online-work-portfolio-can-help-a-job-search.html.

Morgan, H. *The Infographic Resume: How to Create a Visual Portfolio That Showcases*
Your Skills and Lands the Job. New York: McGraw-Hill, 2014.

Williams, G. "Using a Career Portfolio." Association for Talent Development. October 17, 2012. https://www.td.org/Publications/Blogs/Career-Development-Blog/2012/10/Using-a-Career-Portfolio.

Williams, G., and American Society for Training and Development. *Build Your Training*
Portfolio. Alexandria, VA: American Society for Training & Development, 2009.

Zimmerman, E. "Showcasing Your Work, in an Online Portfolio." *New York*
Times. June 30, 2012. http://www.nytimes.com/2012/07/01/jobs/an-online-portfolio-can-showcase-your-work-career-couch.html.

Section III: Concluding Thoughts

CHAPTER 11

Pulling It All Together: How to Effectively Develop HR Behavioral Competencies

We know that proficiency in HR competencies is the key to effective performance in HR. We know that adults are motivated to learn on their own. We also know that there are many competency-building activities easily available to all HR professionals. Putting this knowledge together to create a plan of self-directed action has been the purpose of this book.

Every individual has a storage tank filled with life and work experiences. This reserve is a valuable and rich resource for learning. If we are to master the HR competencies that we need to do our jobs and be successful in HR, then we need to call up all the resources available to us. Adult learning theories tells us that we each want to be involved in the planning, evaluation, and execution of learning activities. Our experience and the experience of others—even the mistakes we've made or witnessed—can provide a rich basis for learning.

Embracing the notion that the potential for learning is all around us provides each of us with a greater array of learning possibilities. Benjamin Franklin said, "Tell me and I forget, teach me and I may remember, involve me and I learn."[1] Our lesson for developing HR competencies is that incidental learning should be used to our advantage and kept at the forefront of our day-to-day activities. Stay involved with your learning and with your career. Figure 11.1 provides a view of how the self-managed activities identified in this book work in concert with professional development and any credentials you may have or obtain to

FIGURE 11.1 HR COMPETENCY DEVELOPMENT: A PROCESS FOR SELF-MANAGED DEVELOPMENT

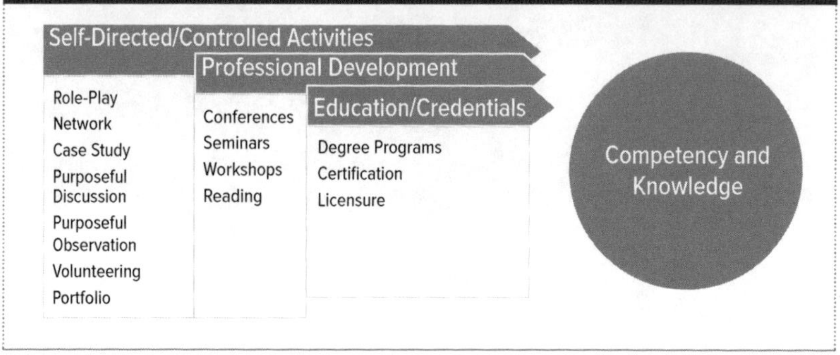

Self-Directed/Controlled Activities

Professional Development

Education/Credentials

Role-Play	Conferences	Degree Programs
Network	Seminars	Certification
Case Study	Workshops	Licensure
Purposeful Discussion	Reading	
Purposeful Observation		
Volunteering		
Portfolio		

Competency and Knowledge

lead to competency and knowledge in HR. The figure does not suggest you must do each item listed, but it is clear that the more you do and the more you focus on the activities identified, the more potential you have for demonstrating your personal competency as an HR professional.

The most important next steps for you will be to build a plan for yourself or to set goals for your competency development. At this point, it may be beneficial to think about short- and long-term goals with respect to which competencies you need to focus on now and how to prioritize your approach. These will likely need to be rotated on and off your priority list depending on what role or assignments are central to you at any given time. The more specific and measurable your goals, the more likely it will be to attain them. Table 11.1 can be used to create a specific vision for each behavioral competency and then a related set of goals to enable you to achieve the development you need to meet the vision you've set.

Think about your competency development from both a strategic and holistic perspective. Given the value in interrelatedness of HR behavioral competencies, you should be comprehensive in your approach. Look for opportunities to develop multiple behavioral competencies at one time, and think in advance of how to measure your progress. The table provides a mechanism for you to do this. Keep in mind that although the suggestion in this book is for self-directed learning, you are not alone in your journey. Other HR professionals are on the same or similar journeys, and those to whom you report all have vested interests in seeing you be successful in your development and personal evolution.

The more successful we are as HR professionals and the more we develop our HR competencies, the better it is for the HR profession overall—and

TABLE 11.1 SETTING YOUR INDIVIDUAL COMPETENCY GOALS

Instructions: Prepare a vision statement for each behavioral competency. Create specific goals, actions, time-frames, and resources needed for each. Consider starting with two or three of the competencies rather than all eight. Or, if you do create goals for all eight, consider prioritizing the competency development goals so you focus on just a few at a time.

[Competency here] Vision Statement:

Development Goal	Development Actions	Timeframe	Resources Needed	Status

the stronger we are viewed, the stronger the profession will be viewed. As we move from or between the roles of HR professionals to HR leaders, we must continuously think of the profession and how we can advance how HR is viewed. Make it your personal mission to help others see how strong and valuable HR is to an organization's success. Individually and collectively, we are the future of the profession.

In addition to the specific learning activities highlighted in this book, you can take a variety of other self-directed actions to enhance formal learning activities. For example, when you attend conferences and seminars, try building your competencies—not just your knowledge. The following tips may be helpful:

- *Get to know the other participants.* Don't just network; ask them how they handle specific situations. Follow through after the event, and form a lasting relationship built on the common denominator of learning. This should be true even if you don't live in close proximity to the other participants. If you're sitting next to someone in the class, at lunch, or in a common area—engage him or her!

- *Establish a rapport with the presenters.* If they are amenable, keep in touch. Use their name. Remind them of your name. Look for things in common, and ask for advice about additional information on the topic of the course. This way, the presenters are more likely to remember you, and you never know what may come of the connection.

- *Ask questions during the session.* Don't err on the side of asking too many questions, but do try to go beyond the content and ask about application of the content to help build your skills. Purposeful discussion can enrich your seminar or conference experience.

- *Look for role-play and case-study scenarios* while in the session(s). Keep a running list of ideas, and create the details while you are at the training session/conference.

- *Spend some time observing attendees and the presenters.* These are new people for you to experience and in a new environment. Take advantage of their different perspectives.

- *Ask others how they plan to build their expertise* in the subject/content of the training. Look for and capture a variety of ideas. Ask others about their goals with respect to the topic—not to copy them, but to learn more about their challenges and how they may be similar or different from your challenges. In addition to enhanced learning available through a conference or seminar, there are many other self-directed learning activities to consider and use.

Other self-directed activities to consider include the following:

- Read books, articles, and other material for gateways to information, relevant stories, and other valuable data.

- Look for and *watch* YouTube videos or others available on the Internet. For example, if you search "how to handle difficult situations," you will be met with a long list of vignettes to watch. The videos can be filtered by length, date, features, and so forth. Not all will be helpful or relevant, but some may spark your own thinking about how to handle certain situations. The more specific you are with your search, the more likely you are to find a vignette that can offer something useful for you and other colleagues to discuss.

- Create a *book club* with other professionals both inside and outside of HR. Select a variety of business, management, and leadership books. Discuss the implications and applications of the key points. Rotate responsibility for leading the discussion and creating questions for the group.[2]

- Form a *movie club* and select movies that have interesting behavioral implications and that can be discussed. Some examples may include:

  ‹ The Wolf of Wall Street
  ‹ The Big Short

- Create a *competency development discussion group* as part of your local professional organization, such as a local Society for Human Resource Management chapter or another group. You have many options when forming a discussion group; for example, it could be organized by level, it could be held independent of meetings, it could begin 40 minutes before the chapter meeting, and so on.

- Create a small *breakfast club* with the purpose of discussing specific issues with a behavioral focus. Form this with just a few other people, and actively bring in guests each month to infuse the group with new ideas and perspectives.

- Create a *Facebook page* for HR competencies where people can post examples of positive proficiency statements or ask questions about how to handle certain situations.

- Post relevant discussion questions on LinkedIn about one or two competencies that you want, or need, to develop and then observe and moderate the discussion.

- Reverse mentor someone far senior to you (either inside or outside of HR) in a skill like using social media; you will derive the benefit of learning from his or her experience during the exchanges.

Learning new things is fun, and being able to do new and different things can be rewarding. Think about the new skills and capabilities you've been developing by following the suggestions in this book. Each of the self-directed activities detailed in this book will not make you a superior HR professional. Taken together, however, the concepts in this book show you that being aware of your own competency level and focusing on developing your HR behavioral competencies are ways to distinguish yourself as a competent and high-performing HR professional. You can learn and develop behavioral competencies every day—focusing on this will set you apart.

How to Measure Success and What to Do Next

There are many ways to measure the success of your efforts and to focus on development. Informal measurements include positive feedback received from HR leaders, HR colleagues, and peers from other functions across your organization. More formal measurements comprise promotions, accolades for achievements, or opportunities for projects and task assignments that are of interest. An effective way to measure your accomplishments is by using the worksheets throughout the book—and those you might develop for yourself. The tools in this book are designed to help you think through and practice setting goals for personal development with respect to behavioral competencies. Ultimately, by immersing yourself in the process of being focused on behavioral development, in addition to HR technical development, self-directed learning will become second nature to you and will not require worksheets or as much organizational effort. Therefore, a measure of success will be when you recognize that your thinking and approach to the eight behavioral competencies are ingrained in your everyday life. There may not be one single measure that demonstrates this achievement, but it will become a way of professional life, and you will see the difference in both your career and your business interactions.

If you are not yet certified, the ultimate measure of success on developing behavioral competencies would be to obtain your SHRM-CP or SHRM-SCP certification. Unlike degree programs, the SHRM certifications require that you not only know technical HR—but that you are able to demonstrate that you practice HR effectively by being able to respond to competency-based questions. Any time you take an exam or evaluation, it is a good idea to prepare. However, in the case of a competency-based certification, the more expertise you have and the greater your ability to apply your knowledge to specific situations, the more likely you will have success in obtaining that certification. Following the steps in this book may well help you prepare to be successful in the SHRM certification process. Obtaining certifications is a direct and visible way to demonstrate the success of your efforts. In addition, some of the activities suggested in this book can lead to activities that will be worthy of recertification credits. Regardless, a focus on behaviors and the development of effective behaviors will serve you well throughout your career.

The analogy to dieting at the start of the book applies here as well. You need the right tools, resources, and motivation to be successful in dieting. More importantly, you need to establish for yourself a new way of eating. With respect to competency development, we need the right tools, resources, and motivation, and we must also establish a new way of thinking about our competency development such that it is part of our everyday approach to working and interacting with those around us. For some, this may be quite easy, or as with dieting, less "necessary," but for most, it will need to be in the forefront of everyday decisions and everyday actions. Think about the following as you continue your career in HR—no matter what level you are or what level to which you aspire:

- Find the right balance of formal professional development and self-directed learning.
- Make it about your personal and continuous development and not just about a promotion or a single goal.
- Establish routines for yourself that include self-initiated activities from single one-time actions to habits that become part of your career lifestyle.
- Establish a group of go-to colleagues who can assist you and whom you can assist as you all develop your behavioral competencies for work and personal effectiveness.

A focus on HR *behavioral* competencies is here to stay, and the more we make it a way of life for development and action, the more successful we will be, and the more successful we will be at helping others going forward.

Additional Reading for All HR Competencies

Appendix A: Additional Reading for All HR Competencies[1]

This collection of resources is provided as a guide and is broken down by level and by the nine competencies (one technical expertise—identified below as "HR Expertise"—and eight behavioral). Note that there are redundancies in the list because some of the resources cover multiple HR behavioral competencies.

Early Level

- Is a specialist in a specific support function, or is a generalist with limited experience.
- Holds a formal title such as HR assistant, junior recruiter, or benefits clerk.

HR Expertise

The ability to apply the principles and practices of HR management to contribute to the success of the business.

Green, Pamela J. *HR: Lead, Achieve, and Succeed in HR.* Washington, DC: Westcom Press, 2011.

Mondore, Scott P., Shane S. Douthitt, and Marisa A. Carson. *Business-Focused HR: 11 Processes to Drive Results.* Alexandria, VA: Society for Human Resource Management, 2011.

SHRM Essentials of HR Management (online learning and workbook system).

Business Acumen

The ability to understand and apply information to contribute to the organization's strategic plan.

Cope, Kevin. *Seeing the Big Picture: Business Acumen to Build Your Credibility, Career, and Company.* Austin: Greenleaf Book Group Press, 2012.

Hock, Randolph. *The Extreme Searcher's Internet Handbook: A Guide for the Serious Searcher*, 4th ed. Medord, NJ: Information Today, 2013.

Silbiger, Steven A. *The Ten-Day MBA: A Step-by-Step Guide to Mastering the Skills Taught In America's Top Business Schools*, 4th ed. New York: HarperBusiness, 2012.

Communication

The ability to effectively exchange with stakeholders.

Alred, Gerald J., Charles T. Brusaw, and Walter E. Oliu. *The Business Writer's Handbook*, 10th ed. New York: St. Martin Press, 2012.

Buhler, Patricia M., and Joel D. Worden. *Up, Down, and Sideways: High-Impact Verbal Communication for HR Professionals.* Alexandria, VA: Society for Human Resource Management.

Duarte, Nancy. *HBR Guide to Persuasive Presentations.* Boston: Harvard Business Press, 2012.

Halvorson, Heidi Grant. *No One Understands You and What to Do About It.* Boston: Harvard Business School Publishing, 2015.

Quintanilla, Kelly M., and Shawn T. Wahl. *Business and Professional Communication: Keys for Workplace Excellence*, 3rd ed. Thousand Oaks, CA: Sage 2017.

Reynolds, Garr. *Presentation Zen: Simple Ideas on Presentation Design and Delivery*, 2nd ed. Berkeley, CA: New Riders, 2011.

Consultation

The ability to provide guidance to organizational stakeholders.

Andersen, Erika. *Be Bad First: Get Good at Things Fast to Stay Ready for the Future.* Brookline, MA: Bibliomotion, 2016.

Gawande, Atul. *The Checklist Manifesto: How to Get Things Right*. New York: Metropolitan Books, 2010.

Rowe, Sandra F. *Project Management for Small Projects*, 2nd ed. Vienna, VA: Management Concepts, 2015.

Sobel, Andrew, and Jerold Panas. *Power Questions: Build Relationships, Win New Business, and Influence Others*. Hoboken, NJ: Wiley, 2012.

Critical Evaluation

The ability to interpret information to make business decisions and recommendations.

Browne, M. Neil, and Stuart M. Keeley. *Asking the Right Questions: A Guide to Critical Thinking*, 11th ed. London: Longman, 2014.

Burger, Edward B., and Michael Starbird. *The 5 Elements of Effective Thinking*. Princeton, NJ: Princeton University Press, 2012.

Fitz-enz, Jac. *The New HR Analytics: Predicting the Economic Value of Your Company's Human Capital Investments*. New York: AMACOM, 2010.

Ethical Practice

The ability to support and uphold the values of the organization while mitigating risk.

Bazerman, Max H., and Ann E. Tenbrunsel. *Blind Spots: Why We Fail to Do What's Right and What to Do about It*. Princeton, NJ: Princeton University Press, 2012.

Hartman, Laura, Joseph DesJardins, and Chris MacDonald. *Business Ethics: Decision Making for Personal Integrity & Social Responsibility*, 3rd ed. New York: McGraw-Hill/Irwin, 2013.

Howard, Ronald A., and Clinton D. Korver. *Ethics for the Real World: Creating a Personal Code to Guide Decisions in Work and Life*. Boston: Harvard Business Review Press, 2008.

Weinstein, Bruce D. *The Good Ones: Ten Crucial Qualities of High-Character Employees*. Novato, CA: New World Library, 2015.

Global and Cultural Effectiveness

The ability to value and consider the perspectives and backgrounds of all parties.

Banaji, Mahzarin R., and Anthony G. Greenwald. *Blindspot: Hidden Biases of Good People*. New York: Delacorte Press, 2013.

Bucher, Richard D. Diversity Consciousness: Opening our Minds to People, Cultures and Opportunities, 3rd ed. Upper Saddle River, NJ: Prentice Hall, 2010.

Krznaric, Roman. *Empathy: Why It Matters, and How to Get It*. New York: Penguin, 2014.

Markus, Hazel Rose, and Alana Conner. *Clash!: How to Thrive in a Multicultural World*. New York: Plume, 2014.

Molinsky, Andrew. *Global Dexterity: How to Adapt Your Behavior Across Cultures without Losing Yourself in the Process*. Boston: Harvard Business Press, 2013.

Ross, Howard J. *Everyday Bias: Identifying and Navigating Unconscious Judgments in Our Daily Lives*. Lanham, MD: Rowman & Littlefield, 2014.

Leadership and Navigation

The ability to direct and contribute to initiatives and processes within the organization.

HBR Guide to Managing Up and Across. Boston: Harvard Business Review Press, 2013.

Ibarra, Herminia. *Act Like a Leader, Think Like a Leader*. Boston: Harvard Business Review Press, 2015.

Kaplan, Robert Steven. *What You Really Need to Lead: The Power of Thinking and Acting Like an Owner*. Boston: Harvard Business Review Press, 2015.

King, Sara N., David Altman, and Robert J. Lee. *Discovering the Leader in You: How to Realize Your Leadership Potential*, New and Revised. San Francisco: Jossey-Bass, 2011.

Wheelan, Susan A. *Creating Effective Teams: A Guide for Members and Leaders*, 4th ed. Thousand Oaks, CA: Sage, 2013.

Relationship Management

The ability to manage interactions to provide service and to support the organization.

Bradberry, Travis, and Jean Greaves. *Emotional Intelligence 2.0*. San Diego: TalentSmart, 2009.

Curtin, Steve. *Delight Your Customers: 7 Simple Ways to Raise Your Customer*

Service from Ordinary to Extraordinary. New York: AMACOM, 2013.

Markova, Dawna, and Angie McArthur. *Collaborative Intelligence: Thinking with People Who Think Differently*. New York: Spiegel & Grau, 2015.

Patterson, Kerry, et al. *Crucial Conversations: Tools for Talking When Stakes Are High*, 2nd ed. New York: McGraw-Hill, 2011.

Seglin, Jeffrey L. *The Simple Art of Business Etiquette: How to Rise to the Top by Playing Nice*. Berkeley, CA: Tycho, 2015.

Mid Level

- Is a generalist, or is a senior specialist.
- Manages projects or programs.
- Holds a formal title such as HR manager, generalist, or senior specialist.

HR Expertise

The ability to apply the principles and practices of human resource management to contribute to the success of the business.

Holbeche, Linda. *Aligning Human Resources and Business Strategy*, 2nd ed. Burlington, MA: Butterworth-Heinemann, 2009.

Latham, Gary P. *Becoming the Evidence-Based Manager: Making the Science of Management Work for You*. Boston: Nicholas Brealey America and Society for Human Resource Management, 2011.

Vogelsang, John, et al., eds. *Handbook for Strategic HR: Best Practices in Organization Development from the OD Network*. New York: AMACOM, 2012.

Business Acumen

The ability to understand and apply information to contribute to the organization's strategic plan.

Anderson, Carol E. M. *Repurposing HR: From a Cost Center to a Business Accelerator*. Alexandria, VA: Society for Human Resource Management, 2015.

Berman, Karen, Joe Knight, and John Case. *Financial Intelligence for HR Professionals*. Boston: Harvard Business School Press, 2008.

Garey, Regan W. *Business Literacy Survival Guide for HR Professionals*. Alexandria, VA: Society for Human Resource Management, 2011.

Hock, Randolph. *The Extreme Searcher's Internet Handbook: A Guide for the Serious Searcher*, 4th ed. Medord, NJ: Information Today, 2013.

Kaiser, Kevin M., Michael Pich, and I. J. Schecter. *Becoming a Top Manager: Tools and Lessons in Transitioning to General Management*. San Francisco: Jossey-Bass, 2015.

Communication

The ability to effectively exchange with stakeholders.

Buhler, Patricia M., and Joel D. Worden. *Up, Down, and Sideways: High-Impact Verbal Communication for HR Professionals*. Alexandria, VA: Society for Human Resource Management.

Burg, Bob. *Adversaries into Allies: Win People Over without Manipulation or Coercion*. New York: Portfolio/Penguin, 2013.

Duarte, Nancy. *HBR Guide to Persuasive Presentations*. Boston: Harvard Business Press, 2012.

Halvorson, Heidi Grant. *No One Understands You and What to Do About It*. Boston: Harvard Business School Publishing, 2015.

Quintanilla, Kelly M., and Shawn T Wahl. *Business and Professional Communication: Keys for Workplace Excellence*, 3rd ed. Thousand Oaks, CA: Sage, 2017.

Sheen, Raymond, and Amy Gallo. *HBR Guide to Building Your Business Case*. Boston: Harvard Business Review Press, 2015.

Stone, Douglas, and Sheila Heen. *Thanks for the Feedback: The Science and Art of Receiving Feedback Well*. New York: Viking, 2014.

Consultation

The ability to provide guidance to organizational stakeholders.

Anderson, Erika. *Be Bad First: Get Good at Things Fast to Stay Ready for the Future*. Brookline, MA: Bibliomotion, 2016.

Galinsky, Adam D., and Maurice Schweitzer. *Friend & Foe: When to Cooperate, When to Compete, and How to Succeed at Both*. New York: Crown Business, 2015.

Gawande, Atul. *The Checklist Manifesto: How to Get Things Right*. New York: Metropolitan Books, 2010.

Goulston, Mark. *Just Listen: Discover the Secret to Getting through to Absolutely Anyone*. New York: AMACOM, 2009.

Green, Charles H., and Andrea P. Howe. *The Trusted Advisor Fieldbook: A Comprehensive Toolkit for Leading with Trust*. Hoboken, NJ: Wiley, 2011.

Klimoski, R., Dugan, B., Messikomer, C., Chiocchio, F. (Eds.), *Advancing Human Resource Project Management*. San Francisco: Jossey-Bass, 2014.

Rowe, Sandra F. *Project Management for Small Projects*, 2nd ed. Vienna, VA: Management Concepts, 2015.

Sawyer, Keith. *Zig Zag: The Surprising Path to Greater Creativity*. San Francisco: Jossey-Bass, 2013.

Critical Evaluation

The ability to interpret information to make business decisions and recommendations.

Browne, M. Neil, and Stuart M. Keeley. *Asking the Right Questions: A Guide to Critical Thinking*, 11th ed. London: Longman, 2014.

Davenport, Thomas H., and Jinho Kim. *Keeping Up with the Quants: Your Guide to Understanding and Using Analytics*. Boston: Harvard Business Review Press, 2013.

Kallet, Michael. *Think Smarter: Critical Thinking to Improve Problem-Solving and Decision-Making Skills*. New York: Wiley, 2014.

Ethical Practice

The ability to support and uphold the values of the organization while mitigating risk.

Bazerman, Max H., and Ann E. Tenbrunsel. *Blind Spots: Why We Fail to Do What's Right and What to Do about It*. Princeton, NJ: Princeton University Press, 2012.

Ferrell, O. C., John Fraedrich, and Linda Ferrell. *Business Ethics: Ethical Decision Making & Cases*, 11th ed. Stamford, CT: Cengage Learning, 2016.

Hartman, Laura, Joseph DesJardins, and Chris MacDonald. *Business Ethics: Decision Making for Personal Integrity & Social Responsibility*, 3rd ed. New York: McGraw-Hill/Irwin, 2013.

Weinstein, Bruce D. *The Good Ones: Ten Crucial Qualities of High-Character*

Employees. Novato, CA: New World Library, 2015.

Global and Cultural Effectiveness

The ability to value and consider the perspectives and backgrounds of all parties.

Banaji, Mahzarin R., and Anthony G. Greenwald. *Blindspot: Hidden Biases of Good People*. New York: Delacorte Press, 2013.

Chaney, Lillian H., and Jeanette S. Martin. *Intercultural Business Communication*, 6th ed. New York: Pearson, 2014.

Davis, Shirley, and Eric Peterson. *Charting Your Path to Success: Key Leadership Competencies Diversity & Inclusion Practitioners Should Have* (DVD). Alexandria, VA: Society for Human Resource Management, 2011.

Krznaric, Roman. *Empathy: Why It Matters, and How to Get It*. New York: Penguin, 2014.

Markus, Hazel Rose, and Alana Conner. *Clash!: How to Thrive in a Multicultural World*. New York: Plume, 2014.

Mor Barak, Michálle E. *Managing Diversity: Toward a Globally Inclusive Workplace*, 3rd ed. Thousand Oaks, CA: Sage.

Ross, Howard J. *Everyday Bias: Identifying and Navigating Unconscious Judgments in Our Daily Lives*. Lanham, MD: Rowman & Littlefield, 2014.

Leadership and Navigation

The ability to direct and contribute to initiatives and processes within the organization.

Brosseau, Denise. *Ready to Be a Thought Leader: How to Increase Your Influence, Impact, and Success*. San Francisco: Jossey-Bass, 2014.

Grenny, Joseph, et al. *Influencer: The New Science of Leading Change*, 2nd ed. New York: McGraw-Hill, 2013.

Ibarra, Herminia. *Act Like a Leader, Think Like a Leader*. Boston: Harvard Business Review Press, 2015.

Kaplan, Robert Steven. *What You Really Need to Lead: The Power of Thinking and Acting Like an Owner*. Boston: Harvard Business Review Press, 2015.

Pfeffer, Jeffrey. *Power: Why Some People Have It and Others Don't*. New York: HarperBusiness, 2010.

Watkins, Michael. *The First 90 Days: Proven Strategies for Getting Up to Speed Faster and Smarter*, updated and expanded. Boston: Harvard Business

Review Press, 2013.

Relationship Management

The ability to manage interactions to provide service and to support the organization.

Cockerell, Lee. *The Customer Rules: The 39 Essential Rules for Delivering Sensational Service*. New York: Crown Business, 2013.

The Essentials of Power, Influence, and Persuasion. Boston: Harvard Business School Press and Society for Human Resource Management, 2006.

Grant, Adam M. *Give and Take: Why Helping Others Drives Our Success*. New York: Penguin, 2014.

Knief, Amanda. *The Citizen Lobbyist: A How-to Manual for Making Your Voice Heard in Government*. Durham, NC: Pitchstone Publishing, 2013.

Markova, Dawna, and Angie McArthur. *Collaborative Intelligence: Thinking with People Who Think Differently*. New York: Spiegel & Grau, 2015.

Morgan, Nick. *Power Cues: The Subtle Science of Leading Groups, Persuading Others, and Maximizing Your Personal Impact*. Boston: Harvard Business Review Press, 2014.

Seglin, Jeffrey L. *The Simple Art of Business Etiquette: How to Rise to the Top by Playing Nice*. Berkeley, CA: Tycho Press, 2015.

Vehar, Jonathan. *Manage Your Boss*. Greensboro, NC: CCL Press, 2016.

Senior Level

- Is an experienced generalist or specialist.
- Holds a formal title such as senior manager, director, or principal.

HR Expertise

The ability to apply the principles and practices of HR management to contribute to the success of the business.

Boudreau, John, and Ravin Jesuthasan. *Transformative HR: How Great Companies Use Evidence-Based Change for Sustainable Advantage*. San Francisco: Jossey-Bass, 2011.

Maitland, Alison, and Peter Thomson. *Future Work: How Businesses Can Adapt and Thrive in the New World of Work*. New York: Palgrave Macmillan, 2011.

Vogelsang, John, et al., eds. *Handbook for Strategic HR: Best Practices in Organization Development from the OD Network*. New York: AMACOM, 2012.

Business Acumen

The ability to understand and apply information to contribute to the organization's strategic plan.

Anderson, Carol E. M. *Repurposing HR: From a Cost Center to a Business Accelerator*. Alexandria, VA: Society for Human Resource Management, 2015.

Ziskin, Ian. *Three: The Human Resources Emerging Executive*. Wiley, 2015.

Director, Steven. *Financial Analysis for HR Managers: Tools for Linking HR Strategy to Business Strategy*. New York: Pearson FT Press, 2012.

Hock, Randolph. *The Extreme Searcher's Internet Handbook: A Guide for the Serious Searcher*, 4th ed. Medord, NJ: Information Today, 2013.

Sharp, Seena. *Competitive Intelligence Advantage: How to Minimize Risk, Avoid Surprises, and Grow Your Business in a Changing World*. New York: Wiley, 2009.

Wright, Lance. *HR in the Boardroom: The HR Professional's Guide to Earning a Place in the C-Suite*. New York: Macmillan, 2015.

Communication

The ability to effectively exchange with stakeholders.

Burger, Edward B., and Michael Starbird. *The 5 Elements of Effective Thinking*. Princeton, NJ: Princeton University Press, 2012.

Halvorson, Heidi Grant. *No One Understands You and What to Do About It*. Boston: Harvard Business School Publishing, 2015.

Fisher, Roger, et al. *Getting to Yes: Negotiating Agreement Without Giving In*. New York: Penguin Books, 2011.

Kouzes, James M., and Barry Z. Posner. *Credibility: How Leaders Gain and Lose It, Why People Demand It*, 2nd ed. San Francisco: Jossey-Bass, 2011.

Kubicek, Jeremie, and Steve Cockram. *5 Voices: How to Communicate Effectively with Everyone You Lead*. New York: Wiley, 2016.

Sheen, Raymond, and Amy Gallo. *HBR Guide to Building Your Business Case*. Boston: Harvard Business Review Press, 2015.

Stone, Douglas, and Sheila Heen. *Thanks for the Feedback: The Science and Art of*

Receiving Feedback Well. New York: Viking, 2014.

Consultation

The ability to provide guidance to organizational stakeholders.

Galinsky, Adam D., and Maurice Schweitzer. *Friend & Foe: When to Cooperate, When to Compete, and How to Succeed at Both.* New York: Crown Business, 2015.

Green, Charles H., and Andrea P. Howe. *The Trusted Advisor Fieldbook: A Comprehensive Toolkit for Leading with Trust.* Hoboken, NJ: Wiley, 2011.

Klimoski, Richard J., et al. *Advancing Human Resource Project Management.* San Francisco: Jossey-Bass, 2014.

Lay, Dwane. *Lean HR: Introducing Process Excellence to Your Practice.* Charleston, SC: CreateSpace, 2013.

Sawyer, Keith. *Zig Zag: The Surprising Path to Greater Creativity.* San Francisco: Jossey-Bass, 2013.

Critical Evaluation

The ability to interpret information to make business decisions and recommendations.

Davenport, Thomas H. *Big Data at Work: Dispelling the Myths, Uncovering the Opportunities.* Boston: Business Review Press, 2014.

Davenport, Thomas H., and Jinho Kim. *Keeping Up with the Quants: Your Guide to Understanding and Using Analytics.* Boston: Harvard Business Review Press, 2013.

Knaflic, Cole Nussbaumer. *Storytelling with Data: A Data Visualization Guide for Business Professionals.* New York: Wiley, 2015.

Pease, Gene, et al. *Human Capital Analytics: How to Harness the Potential of Your Organization's Greatest Asset.* New York: Wiley, 2012.

Provost, Foster, and Tom Fawcett. *Data Science for Business: What You Need to Know about Data Mining and Data-Analytic Thinking.* Sebastopol, CA: O'Reilly, 2013.

Ethical Practice

The ability to support and uphold the values of the organization while mitigating risk.

Bazerman, Max H., and Ann E. Tenbrunsel. *Blind Spots: Why We Fail to Do What's Right and What to Do about It*. Princeton, NJ: Princeton University Press, 2012.

Ferrell, O. C., John Fraedrich, and Linda Ferrell. *Business Ethics: Ethical Decision Making & Cases*, 11th ed. Stamford, CT: Cengage Learning, 2016.

Trevino, Linda K., and Katherine A. Nelson. *Managing Business Ethics: Straight Talk about How to Do It Right*, 6th ed. New York: Wiley, 2013.

Weinstein, Bruce D. *The Good Ones: Ten Crucial Qualities of High-Character Employees*. Novato, CA: New World Library, 2015.

Global and Cultural Effectiveness

The ability to value and consider the perspectives and backgrounds of all parties.

Banaji, Mahzarin R., and Anthony G. Greenwald. *Blindspot: Hidden Biases of Good People*. New York: Delacorte Press, 2013.

Chaney, Lillian H., and Jeanette S. Martin. *Intercultural Business Communication*, 6th ed. New York: Pearson, 2014.

Ferdman, Bernardo M., and Barbara R. Deane, eds. *Diversity at Work: The Practice of Inclusion*. San Francisco: Jossey-Bass, 2013.

Markus, Hazel Rose, and Alana Conner. *Clash!: How to Thrive in a Multicultural World*. New York: Plume, 2014.

Mor Barak, Michálle E. *Managing Diversity: Toward a Globally Inclusive Workplace*, 3rd ed. Thousand Oaks, CA: Sage.

Krznaric, Roman. *Empathy: Why It Matters, and How to Get It*. New York: Penguin, 2014.

Livermore, David. *Leading with Cultural Intelligence: The Real Secret to Success*. New York: American Management Association, 2015.

Meyer, Erin. *The Culture Map: Breaking Through the Invisible Boundaries of Global Business*. New York: PublicAffairs, 2014.

Ross, Howard J. *Everyday Bias: Identifying and Navigating Unconscious Judgments in Our Daily Lives*. Lanham, MD: Rowman & Littlefield, 2014.

Leadership and Navigation

The ability to direct and contribute to initiatives and processes within the organization.

Bradberry, Travis, and Jean Greaves. *Leadership 2.0*. San Diego: TalentSmart,

2012.

Grenny, Joseph, et al. *Influencer: The New Science of Leading Change*, 2nd ed. New York: McGraw-Hill, 2013.

Ulrich, Dave, and Norm Smallwood. *Leadership Sustainability: Seven Disciplines to Achieve the Changes Great Leaders Know They Must Make*. New York: McGraw-Hill, 2013.

Watkins, Michael. *The First 90 Days: Proven Strategies for Getting Up to Speed Faster and Smarter*, updated and expanded. Boston: Harvard Business Review Press, 2013.

Relationship Management

The ability to manage interactions to provide service and to support the organization.

Kaye, Beverly, and Julie Winkle Giulioni. *Help Them Grow or Watch Them Go: Career Conversations Employees Want*. San Francisco: Berrett-Koehler Publishers, 2012.

Kenton, Barbara, and Jane Yarnall. *HR: The Business Partner*, 2nd ed. Oxford, England: Butterworth-Heinemann, 2009.

Knief, Amanda. *The Citizen Lobbyist: A How-to Manual for Making Your Voice Heard in Government*. Durham, NC: Pitchstone Publishing, 2013.

Latham, Gary P., and Robert C. Ford. *HR at Your Service: Lessons from Benchmark Service Organizations*. Alexandria, VA: Society for Human Resource Management, 2012.

Markova, Dawna, and Angie McArthur. *Collaborative Intelligence: Thinking with People Who Think Differently*. New York: Spiegel & Grau, 2015.

Morgan, Nick. *Power Cues: The Subtle Science of Leading Groups, Persuading Others, and Maximizing Your Personal Impact*. Boston: Harvard Business Review Press, 2014.

Schein, Edgar H. *Humble Inquiry: The Gentle Art of Asking Instead of Telling*. San Francisco: Berrett-Koehler Publishers, 2014.

Vehar, Jonathan. *Manage Your Boss*. Greensboro, NC: CCL Press, 2016.

Executive Level

- Typically is one of the most senior leaders in HR.
- Holds the top HR job in the organization or a vice president role.

HR Expertise

The ability to apply the principles and practices of human resource management to contribute to the success of the business.

Boudreau, John, and Ravin Jesuthasan. *Transformative HR: How Great Companies Use Evidence-Based Change for Sustainable Advantage*. San Francisco: Jossey-Bass, 2011.

Tavis, Anna, et al., eds. *Point Counterpoint: New Perspectives on People & Strategy*. Chicago: Human Resource Planning Society and Society for Human Resource Management, 2012.

Wright, Patrick M., et al., eds. *The Chief HR Officer: Defining the New Role of Human Resource Leaders*. San Francisco: Jossey-Bass and Society for Human Resource Management, 2011.

Business Acumen

The ability to understand and apply information to contribute to the organization's strategic plan.

Anderson, Carol E. M. *Repurposing HR: From a Cost Center to a Business Accelerator*. Alexandria, VA: Society for Human Resource Management, 2015.

Driving Business Value with Innovative HR Strategies: Leading HR Executives on Leveraging New Technologies and Partnering with the Business to Build a Flexible and Creative Workforce. Boston: Aspatore, 2014.

McCracken, Grant. *Chief Culture Officer: How to Create a Living, Breathing Corporation*. New York: Basic Books, 2009.

Stack, Laura. *Execution Is the Strategy: How Leaders Achieve Maximum Results in Minimum Time*. San Francisco: Berrett-Koehler Publishers, 2014.

Wright, Lance. *HR in the Boardroom: The HR Professional's Guide to Earning a Place in the C-Suite*. New York: Macmillan, 2015.

Ziskin, Ian. *Three: The Human Resources Emerging Executive*. Wiley, 2015.

Communication

The ability to effectively exchange with stakeholders.

Hewlett, Sylvia Ann. *Executive Presence: The Missing Link Between Merit and Success*. New York: HarperBusiness, 2014.

Kouzes, James M., and Barry Z. Posner. *Credibility: How Leaders Gain and Lose It, Why People Demand It*, 2nd ed. San Francisco: Jossey-Bass, 2011.

Stone, Douglas, and Sheila Heen. *Thanks for the Feedback: The Science and Art of Receiving Feedback Well*. New York: Viking, 2014.

Consultation

The ability to provide guidance to organizational stakeholders.

The Stanford Executive Briefing DVD Series: Influence and Negotiation. Mill Valley, CA Kantola.

Wiseman, Liz, and Greg McKeown. *Multipliers: How the Best Leaders Make Everyone Smarter*. New York: HarperBusiness, 2010.

Critical Evaluation

The ability to interpret information to make business decisions and recommendations.

Fitz-enz, Jac, and John Mattox, II. *Predictive Analytics for Human Resources*. New York: Wiley, 2014.

Hubbard, Douglas W. *How to Measure Anything: Finding the Value of Intangibles in Business*, 3rd ed. New York: Wiley, 2014.

Knaflic, Cole Nussbaumer. *Storytelling with Data: A Data Visualization Guide for Business Professionals*. New York: Wiley, 2015.

Provost, Foster, and Tom Fawcett. *Data Science for Business: What You Need to Know about Data Mining and Data-Analytic Thinking*. Sebastopol, CA: O'Reilly, 2013.

Reeves, Martin, Knut Haanaes, and Jammejaya Sinha. *Your Strategy Needs a Strategy: How to Choose and Execute the Right Approach*. Boston: Harvard Business School Publishing, 2015.

Sesil, James C. *Applying Advanced Analytics to HR Management Decisions: Methods for Selection, Developing Incentives, and Improving Collaboration*. Upper Saddle River, NJ: Pearson FT Press, 2013.

Ethical Practice

The ability to support and uphold the values of the organization while mitigating risk.

Bazerman, Max H., and Ann E. Tenbrunsel. *Blind Spots: Why We Fail to Do What's Right and What to Do about It*. Princeton, NJ: Princeton University Press, 2012.

Blakey, John. *The Trusted Executive: Nine Leadership Habits that Inspire Results, Relationships and Reputation*. London: Kogan Page, 2016.

Muir, Ian. *The Tone From the Top: How Behaviour Trumps Strategy*. New York: Gower, 2015.

Steinberg, Richard M. *Governance, Risk Management, and Compliance: It Can't Happen to Us—Avoiding Corporate Disaster While Driving Success*. New York: Wiley, 2011.

Weinstein, Bruce D. *The Good Ones: Ten Crucial Qualities of High-Character Employees*. Novato, CA: New World Library, 2015.

Wulf, Katharina. *Ethics and Compliance Programs in Multinational Organizations*. Berlin, Germany: Gabler Verlag, 2012.

Global and Cultural Effectiveness

The ability to value and consider the perspectives and backgrounds of all parties.

Banaji, Mahzarin R., and Anthony G. Greenwald. *Blindspot: Hidden Biases of Good People*. New York: Delacorte Press, 2013.

Gundling, Ernest, Christie Caldwell, and Karen Cvitkovich. *Leading Across New Borders: How to Succeed as the Center Shifts*. New York: Wiley, 2015.

Krznaric, Roman. *Empathy: Why It Matters, and How to Get It*. New York: Penguin, 2014.

Livermore, David. *Leading with Cultural Intelligence: The Real Secret to Success*. New York: American Management Association, 2015.

Markus, Hazel Rose, and Alana Conner. *Clash!: How to Thrive in a Multicultural World*. New York: Plume, 2014.

Meyer, Erin. *The Culture Map: Breaking Through the Invisible Boundaries of Global Business*. New York: PublicAffairs, 2014.

Phillips, Patricia Pulliam, and Jack J. Phillips. *Measuring ROI in Employee Relations and Compliance: Case Studies in Diversity and Inclusion, Engagement, Compliance, and Flexible Working Arrangements*. Alexandria, VA: Society for Human Resource Management, 2014.

Ross, Howard J. *Everyday Bias: Identifying and Navigating Unconscious Judgments in Our Daily Lives*. Lanham, MD: Rowman & Littlefield, 2014.

Ross, Howard J. *Reinventing Diversity: Transforming Organizational Community to Strengthen People, Purpose, and Performance.* Lanham, MD: Rowman & Littlefield Publishers, 2013.

Leadership and Navigation

The ability to direct and contribute to initiatives and processes within the organization.

Holbeche, Linda. *HR Leadership.* Burlington, MA: Butterworth-Heinemann, 2009.

Ulrich, Dave, and Norm Smallwood. *Leadership Sustainability: Seven Disciplines to Achieve the Changes Great Leaders Know They Must Make.* New York: McGraw-Hill, 2013.

Relationship Management

The ability to manage interactions to provide service and to support the organization.

Global HR Leadership Strategies: Leading HR Executives on Managing Talent, Supporting Business Goals, and Driving Company Culture in an Evolving Global Environment. Boston: Aspatore, 2013.

Hansen, Morten. *Collaboration: How Leaders Avoid the Traps, Build Common Ground, and Reap Big Results.* Boston: Harvard Business Review Press, 2009.

Manning, Harley, and Kerry Bodine. *Outside In: The Power of Putting Customers at the Center of Your Business.* Harley 2012. Las Vegas: Amazon Publishing/ New Harvest, 2012.

Markova, Dawna, and Angie McArthur. *Collaborative Intelligence: Thinking with People Who Think Differently.* New York: Spiegel & Grau, 2015.

Schein, Edgar H. *Humble Inquiry: The Gentle Art of Asking Instead of Telling.* San Francisco: Berrett-Koehler Publishers, 2014.

Development of the SHRM Competency Model

Appendix B: Development of the SHRM Competency Model

The SHRM Competency Model was rigorously created over several years. The intent of the model was to provide a basis on which HR professionals can learn, develop, and grow. The Competency Model is fundamental to the HR profession because it will help develop HR professional at all levels of the organization regardless of one's position. The model is an excellent source for understanding career growth and career potential. The SHRM Competency Model sets out a framework for identifying and understanding what HR professionals need to be able to *do* (i.e., actions and behaviors) to be successful and drive organizational value and success.[1]

The SHRM Competency Model is designed to provide HR professionals with a *blueprint* to increase their abilities and performance on the job—at all levels in their career. The competencies and behavioral proficiencies contained in the model focus on how HR professionals can be proficient and achieve valuable results. In many ways, the Competency Model can be used as a personal professional development plan, and it can be customized for HR professionals once they know or assess their competency in any one of the nine stated behavioral competencies.[2]

SHRM spoke directly with more than 1,200 HR professionals in the U.S. and abroad to develop the model, which was then tested and validated with more than 32,000 HR professionals. Further, the model has gone through criterion validation with 1,300 HR professionals and 900 of their direct supervisors. For more detail about the model, the content validation, and criterion validation, visit the following site: www.shrm.org/hrcompetencies

The SHRM Competency Model has several characteristics that make it an excellent framework for a career roadmap. First, the model applies to the broad HR profession and describes what each competency looks like at four different career levels—entry, mid, senior, and executive. Second, the model is applicable to any industry or to any HR professional regardless of the size of the organization. The competencies, therefore, transcend industry and organization size and are designed to advance the HR profession. Moreover, the model is global in its focus and development. The purpose of the model is to define success as an HR professional and, therefore, provide a guide of how to attain success. The proficiency statements or standards in the model offer relevant guidance to HR professionals on what they need to be able to do. A proficiency standard is a statement, developed and validated using input from HR subject matter experts at all career levels. These statements are benchmarks of effective behavior.

Learning opportunities abound, regardless of career level, and can be directed in a way that systematically helps HR professionals become more proficient and more cognizant of the behaviors they employ to be effective in their role. Regardless of whether you are a currently certified HR professional, are intending to pursue competency-based certification, or direct those who are certified or intending to pursue competency-based certification, a focus on competencies will be useful for you. This book will provide prescriptions of how you can develop or help others develop their competencies. Competencies develop overtime, and just like practicing a golf swing or tennis serve, the more you focus on it, the better you will get at execution. Moreover, as a career progresses into other positions and different organizations, your ability to match your competency development to your immediate needs and subsequent needs will be met.

TABLE B.1 OVERVIEW OF BUSINESS ACUMEN

Business Acumen: The ability to understand and apply information to contribute to the organization's strategic plan.

Subcompetencies	Sample Behaviors
• Strategic Agility • Business Knowledge • Systems Thinking • Economic Awareness • Effective Administration • Knowledge of Finance and Accounting • Knowledge of Sales and Marketing • Knowledge of Technology • Knowledge of Labor Markets • Knowledge of Business Operations/ Logistics • Knowledge of Government and Regulatory Guidelines • HR and Organizational Metrics/Analytics/ Business Indicators	• Demonstrates a capacity for understanding the business operations and functions within the organization • Understands the industry and business/ competitive environment within which the organization operates • Makes the business case for HR management as it relates to efficient and effective organizational functioning • Understands organizational metrics and their correlation to business success • Uses organizational resources to learn the business and operational functions • Uses organizational metrics to make decisions • Markets HR both internally (e.g., ROI of HR initiatives) and externally (e.g., employment branding) • Leverages technology to solve business problems

Proficiency Standards by Career Level: Sample standards for each career level

Early Level: Possesses operational/processing expertise for assigned tasks; identifies inefficiencies and provides process improvement recommendations; develops knowledge and understanding of value of cost-benefit analysis.

Mid Level: Analyzes data for HR metrics to make recommendations; manages process improvement initiatives; implements organizationwide business practices/operations.

Senior Level: Benchmarks the competition and other relevant comparison groups; sets policies and procedures/practices to support organizational success; maintains a systems-thinking perspective when making business decisions.

Executive Level: Benchmarks the competition and other relevant comparison groups; develops HR business strategies to drive key business results; sets HR and business technology strategy to solve business problems and needs.

For additional proficiency standards at each level visit: www.shrm.org/hrcompetencies.

Developing Proficiency in HR: 7 Self-Directed Activities for HR Professionals

TABLE B.2 OVERVIEW OF COMMUNICATION	
Communication: The ability to effectively exchange information with stakeholders.	
Subcompetencies	**Sample Behaviors**
• Verbal Communication Skills • Written Communication Skills • Presentation Skills • Persuasion • Diplomacy • Perceptual Objectivity • Active Listening • Effective Timely Feedback • Facilitation Skills • Meeting Effectiveness • Social Technology and Social Media Savvy • Public Relations	• Listens actively and empathetically to the views of others • Delivers critical information to all stakeholders • Seeks further information to clarify ambiguity • Provides constructive feedback effectively • Ensures effective communication throughout the organization • Provides thoughtful feedback in appropriate situations • Provides proactive communications • Demonstrates an understanding of the audience's perspective • Treats constructive feedback as a developmental opportunity • Welcomes the opportunity to discuss competing points of view • Helps others consider new perspectives • Leads effective and efficient meetings • Helps managers communicate not just on HR issues • Utilizes communication technology and social media

Proficiency Standards by Career Level: Sample standards for each career level

Early Level: Produces accurate and error-free communication; produces top quality reports and documents; communicates policies, procedures, culture, etc., to new and existing employees.

Mid Level: Delivers well-organized, impactful presentations; translates organizational communication strategies into practice at the operational level; delivers constructive feedback.

Senior Level: Disseminates HR and other executives' messages to stakeholders; creates channels for open communication across and within levels of responsibility; oversees culture communication strategy.

Executive Level: Articulates the alignment between organizational HR initiatives and organizational strategy; communicates the corporate mission and vision to other stakeholders; delivers strategic messages supporting HR and business.

For additional proficiency standards at each level visit: www.shrm.org/hrcompetencies.

TABLE B.3 OVERVIEW OF CONSULTATION

Consultation: The ability to provide guidance to organizational stakeholders.

Subcompetencies	Sample Behaviors
• Coaching • Project Management (Vision, Design, Implementation, and Evaluation) • Analytic Reasoning • Problem-solving • Inquisitiveness • Creativity and Innovation • Flexibility • Respected Business Partner • Career Pathing/Talent Management/People Management • Time Management	• Applies creative problem-solving to address business needs and issues • Serves as an in-house workforce and people management expert • Analyzes specific business challenges involving the workforce and offers solutions based upon best practice or research • Generates specific organizational interventions (e.g., culture change, change management, restructuring, training) to support organizational objectives • Develops consultative and coaching skills • Guides employees regarding specific career situations

Proficiency Standards by Career Level: Sample standards for each career level

Early Level: Conducts initial investigation for HR-based transactional issues; gathers and, when appropriate, analyzes facts and data for business solutions; identifies stakeholder needs and refers as appropriate.

Mid Level: Conducts initial investigation of HR issues; evaluates and measures current processes; manages projects within allotted time and budget.

Senior Level: Provides guidance to managers and business unit teams; ensures that HR and business solutions are on time, on budget, and high quality; designs creative business solutions utilizing HR expertise/perspective.

Executive Level: Listens to business leaders' challenges; develops vision for critical solutions to organizational human capital challenges; uses appropriate analytic tools to provide other leaders input on strategic decisions.

For additional proficiency standards at each level visit: www.shrm.org/hrcompetencies.
Executive Level: Articulates the alignment between organizational HR initiatives and organizational strategy; communicates the corporate mission and vision to other stakeholders; delivers strategic messages supporting HR and business.

For additional proficiency standards at each level visit: www.shrm.org/hrcompetencies.

TABLE B.4 OVERVIEW OF CRITICAL EVALUATION

Critical Evaluation: The ability to interpret information to make business decisions and recommendations.

Subcompetencies	Sample Behaviors
• Measurement and Assessment Skills • Objectivity • Critical Thinking • Problem-solving • Curiosity and Inquisitiveness • Research Methodology • Decision-making • Auditing Skills • Knowledge Management	• Makes sound decisions based on evaluation of available information • Assesses the impact of changes to law on organizational human resource management functions • Transfers knowledge and best practices from one situation to the next • Applies critical thinking to information received from organizational stakeholders and evaluates what can be used for organizational success • Gathers critical information • Analyzes data with a keen sense for what is useful • Analyzes information to identify evidence-based best practices • Identifies leading indicators of outcomes • Analyzes large quantities of information from research and practice

Proficiency Standards by Career Level: Sample standards for each career level

Early Level: Reports on data entry and key metrics; conducts data entry and tracking of statistics and metrics; collects and synthesizes data through surveys, focus groups, research, and other methods.

Mid Level: Asks critical questions to prepare and interpret data studies/metrics; identifies patterns in data and raises relevant issues to higher-level management; analyzes data and seeks root causes.

Senior Level: Possesses advanced knowledge and ability to interpret data and make recommendations; validates processes to ensure that they meet desired and reliable outcomes; identifies critical messages from research, pilot study findings, or best practices.

Executive Level: Utilizes external/environmental awareness and experience in decision-making; challenges assumptions and critically examines all initiatives and programs; provides strategic view to direct and prioritize decision-making.

For additional proficiency standards at each level visit: www.shrm.org/hrcompetencies.

TABLE B.5 OVERVIEW OF ETHICAL PRACTICE

Ethical Practice: The ability to integrate core values, integrity, and accountability throughout all organizational and business practices.

Subcompetencies	Sample Behaviors
• Rapport Building • Trust Building • Personal, Professional, and Behavioral • Integrity • Professionalism • Credibility • Personal and Professional Courage	• Maintains confidentiality • Acts with personal, professional, and behavioral integrity • Responds immediately to all reports of unethical behavior or conflicts of interest • Shows consistency between espoused and enacted values • Acknowledges mistakes • Drives the corporate ethical environment • Applies power or authority appropriately • Maintains appropriate levels of transparency in organizational practices • Ensures that all stakeholder voices are heard • Manages political and social pressures when making decisions

Proficiency Standards by Career Level: Sample standards for each career level

Early Level: Supports training programs regarding ethical laws, standards, and policies; documents and escalates reports of unethical behavior to management; maintains employee confidentiality throughout appropriate business processes.

Mid Level: Establishes oneself as a credible and trustworthy source for employees to voice concerns; influences others to behave in an ethical manner; audits and monitors adherence to policies and procedures.

Senior Level: Oversees processes to protect the confidentiality of employee information; responds promptly and appropriately to reports of unethical behavior; evaluates potential ethical risks and liabilities to the organization.

Executive Level: Withstands politically motivated pressure when developing strategy; maintains a culture that requires all employees to report unethical practices and behavior; aligns all HR practices with ethics, laws, and standards.

For additional proficiency standards at each level visit: www.shrm.org/hrcompetencies.

TABLE B.6 OVERVIEW OF GLOBAL AND CULTURAL EFFECTIVENESS

Global and Cultural Effectiveness: The ability to value and consider the perspectives and backgrounds of all parties.

Subcompetencies	Sample Behaviors
• Global Perspective • Diversity Perspective • Openness to Various Perspectives • Empathy • Openness to Experience • Tolerance for Ambiguity • Adaptability • Cultural Awareness and Respect	• Demonstrates nonjudgmental respect for other perspectives • Works effectively with diverse cultures and populations • Appreciates the commonalities, values, and individual uniqueness of all human beings • Possesses self-awareness and humility to learn from others • Embraces inclusion • Adapts perspective and behavior to meet the cultural context • Operates with a global, open mindset while being sensitive to local cultural issues and needs • Operates with a fundamental trust in other human beings • Incorporates global business and economic trends into business decisions

Proficiency Standards by Career Level: Sample standards for each career level

Early Level: Possesses general knowledge of local cultural issues; respects differences and promotes inclusion on a transactional level; develops some general knowledge of local and global economic trends.

Mid Level: Provides training on culture trends and practices for expatriate workforce; designs, recommends, and/or implements diversity/culture programs; resolves conflicts due to cultural differences.

Senior Level: Develops expert knowledge of global economic trends and best practices; fosters culture of inclusiveness within organization; develops diversity and cultural enhancement programs.

Executive Level: Understands global labor markets and associated legal environments; proves the return on investment of a diverse workforce; builds cross-cultural relationships and partnerships.

For additional proficiency standards at each level visit: www.shrm.org/hrcompetencies.

TABLE B.7 OVERVIEW OF LEADERSHIP AND NAVIGATION

Leadership and Navigation: The ability to direct and contribute to initiatives and processes within the organization.

Subcompetencies	Sample Behaviors
• Transformational and Functional Leadership • Results- and Goal-Oriented • Resource Management • Succession Planning • Project Management • Mission Driven • Change Management • Political Savvy • Influence • Consensus Builder	• Exhibits behaviors consistent with and conforming to organizational culture • Fosters collaboration • Develops solutions to overcome potential obstacles to successful implementation of initiatives • Demonstrates agility and expertise when leading organizational initiatives or when supporting the initiatives of others • Sets the vision for HR initiatives and builds buy-in from internal and external stakeholders • Leads the organization through adversity with resilience and tenacity • Promotes consensus among organizational stakeholders (e.g., employees, business unit leaders) when proposing new initiatives • Serves as a transformational leader for the organization by leading change

Proficiency Standards by Career Level: Sample standards for each career level

Early Level: Listens actively to identify potential challenges or solutions; builds credibility with stakeholders; makes HR transactional decisions within established policies and guidelines.

Mid Level: Supports critical large-scale organizational changes; serves as a point person on projects and tasks; implements plans using results-oriented goals for measuring success.

Senior Level: Establishes programs, policies, and procedures to support the organizational culture; leads project plans for timely completion; manages the resources available effectively to meet planned objectives for initiatives.

Executive Level: Leads HR staff in maintaining or changing organizational culture; identifies the need for and facilitates strategic organizational change; manages risk, opportunities, and gaps in business strategy.

For additional proficiency standards at each level visit: www.shrm.org/hrcompetencies.

TABLE B.8 OVERVIEW OF RELATIONSHIP MANAGEMENT

Relationship Management: The ability to manage interactions to provide service and to support the organization

Subcompetencies	Sample Behaviors
• Business Networking Expertise • Visibility • Customer Service (internal and external) • People Management • Advocacy • Negotiation and Conflict Management • Credibility • Community Relations • Transparency • Proactivity • Responsiveness • Mentorship • Influence • Employee Engagement • Teamwork • Mutual Respect	• Establishes credibility in all interactions • Treats all stakeholders with respect and dignity • Builds engaging relationships with all organizational stakeholders through trust, teamwork, and direct communication • Demonstrates approachability and openness • Ensures alignment within HR when delivering services and information to the organization • Provides customer service to organizational stakeholders • Promotes successful relationships with stakeholders • Champions the view that organizational effectiveness benefits all stakeholders • Serves as an advocate when appropriate • Fosters effective teambuilding among stakeholders

Proficiency Standards by Career Level: Sample standards for each career level

Early Level: Listens effectively to potential issues before reacting with solutions; Serves as frontline liaison with vendors/suppliers; Facilitates the resolution of transactional conflicts that arise.

Mid Level: Oversees transactional and/or preliminary stage of employee relations issues; Mediates difficult interactions, escalating problems to higher level when warranted; Oversees interactions with vendors/suppliers to maintain service quality.

Senior Level: Mediates difficult employee relations and/or other interactions as a neutral party; Builds consensus and settles disputes internal to HR on policy and practice decisions; Facilitates difficult interactions among organizational stakeholders to achieve optimal outcomes.

Executive Level: Designs strategies for improving relationship management performance metrics; Develops and champions organizational customer service strategies and models; Designs strategies to ensure a strong customer service culture in the HR function.

For additional proficiency standards at each level visit: www.shrm.org/hrcompetencies.

Adult Development and Competency Development

Appendix C: Adult Development and Competency Development

It is well known that adults learn differently than children and that different strategies need to be employed to ensure that learning and, more importantly, that the *transfer* of learning into the workplace takes place. Malcolm Knowles (1975 and 1977), an expert in adult learning theory, identified six principles of adult learning that summarize the needs of adults. He stated that:

- Adults are internally motivated and self-directed.
- Adults bring life experiences and knowledge to learning experiences.
- Adults are goal oriented.
- Adults are relevancy oriented.
- Adults are practical.
- Adult learners like to be respected.

In pedagogical learning, the instructor assumes all responsibility for the agenda and what is taught and how it is taught. The instructor is also responsible for evaluating whether learning has taken place. By contrast, adult learners are responsible for their own learning and also are active participants in evaluating whether learning has taken place. Adults can be a rich source of learning for *others*, and the adult learner needs to recognize how to capitalize on this as an opportunity. While students are often told what they have to learn or master, adult learners identify their own gaps in knowledge, skills, abilities, and other characteristics (KSAOs) and seek to remedy gaps of their own accord. As a result, learning is often organized around things that adults need in their professional or personal lives. While there may be external motivations, the ultimate motivation comes from within and drives the adult learner in a particular direction.

Readiness to Learn

Readiness for learning refers to whether a person has the personal characteristics, such as ability, motivation, attitude, or beliefs, needed to learn certain concepts or content and then apply the learning to the workplace or other work environments. Another necessary component is that the work environment needs to facilitate learning so the performance can be demonstrated. Competency development, contrary to employee training, is about how gradual and continuous learning will develop one's competencies. If HR professionals attend a seminar to learn more about the Affordable Care Act (ACA), for example, the purpose is to learn the details of the law and how to comply with the requirements. They need the capacity to learn and apply the information, the motivation to do so, and an organization that is willing to except the need to comply. On the competency side, though, HR professionals need to have the competency to be able to effectively communicate the details of the law as well as the business case for certain approaches. They need to be able to complete critical evaluations of existing benefits plans, costs, and implications and then make relevant recommendations. And they must have the capacity to lead and build relationships with colleagues and employees to gain the buy-in necessary to smoothly implement change with respect to ACA compliance.

Raymond Noe (2009 and 2013), in discussing the learning process, noted that people need to know why they should learn, that they need to use their own experiences as a basis for learning, and that they need to have opportunities for practice. He also noted that feedback is as important as learning by observing and interacting with others. Feedback, to be effective, needs to focus on specific behaviors and should be provided as soon as possible after the behavior has been demonstrated. In developing one's competencies on an ongoing basis, it should be recognized that feedback may come from observing and interacting with others rather than being more formally delivered.

Why Is Self-Directed Learning Important for the Development of HR Competencies?

Self-directed learning is an approach that is successful with most adults. Each of us may have some preferences in how we learn best. We've heard someone say, "I'm a visual learner." Or "I need time to process that." However, a common denominator for adults is interactivity with people and situations. We may process information and experiences differently, but a more active role rather than a passive role with learning will have more of a significant and positive impact. Self-directed learning gives the adult learner control over his or her learning plan. There are numerous benefits and a multitude of reasons why engaging in self-directed learning is important:

- People who take initiative for their own learning are more apt to learn more and learn better. Learning tends to be more permanent and more effective (Knowles).

- Learners dictate what is learned through setting their own goals.

- Learners tailor learning to their needs.

- The approach assumes that learners' own experiences are rich sources for learning and development.

- Learners' motivation is internally driven.

- Learners can become more empowered to take on even more responsibility for their own self-directed development.

Self-directed learning and development does not mean that learning always occurs in isolation or without interaction with others. Learning and development can take the form of a variety of activities and can be found in many settings and through everyday opportunities.

There are many strategies for learning that individuals can employ. We may already do some of these things without labeling them as learning or self-directed activities. For example, we may critique something on our own or volunteer to revise a document or improve on something that already exists. Every time we think of what might be behind a cause and effect relationship or make a prediction about what might occur in a situation, we are essentially creating a learning opportunity for ourselves.

There are numerous ways to develop yourself. The possibilities range from attending conferences or seminars to participating in workshops and retreats—from formal to informal or more self-directed. Your development plan should always include experiences that are more formal and structured. There are a number of the ways to develop.

Possible Ways to Develop

- Distance learning (including *massive open online courses, or* MOOCs).
- Social media.
- Speaking.
- Consulting.
- Leadership and mentoring.
- Internships.
- Volunteer work.
- Role-plays.
- Getting out of your comfort zone.
- Listening and absorbing for learning.
- Asking questions and relevant follow-up questions.
- Presenting and explaining as a way to practice and to receive feedback.
- Doing your homework and being prepared.
- Putting yourself in the shoes of someone you aspire to be.
- Writing a business plan or a strategy document.
- Discussing case scenarios.

These experiences can be even richer if you approach them with an eye toward applying adult learning theory. The more participatory in the process, the better—and the more you network with fellow attendees and instructors, the more effective your learning. For example, if you attend the Society for Human Resource Management annual conference or a local Chamber of Commerce event, plan to ask questions when appropriate, and also plan to engage your fellow participants. Be specific by asking them about their experience or by giving some of your ideas to observe their reaction. Through events and experiences like this, you will be developing a great deal of tacit knowledge that will be applicable in many settings.

It may be tempting to look at the above list and try to assign various approaches to learning to different career levels. Doing so may actually limit an HR professional's opportunities to learn. It's not likely that entry-level professionals will be writing business plans or strategy documents—but participating in the process can certainly offer learning opportunities. Senior leaders can coach learners about approaches to strategic planning and can even highlight the limitations of learners' input to the learner, yet senior leaders may also learn something themselves from the perspective offered by entry-level professionals. On the opposite end of the spectrum, you may think internships are primarily for students or recent graduates. However, I once knew a professor of accountancy who took a sabbatical to accept a six-month internship with one of the large public accounting firms. His contributions (and "learning") were different from a student's, but the goal of doing something to gain experience—the essential definition of an intern—was accomplished. Use Worksheet A.1 and Exercise A.1 to help you think through the adult developmental activities that you've done and the types of activities that most resonate with you. Because adults learn differently, it is important to match your learning preferences with the types of self-directed and professional development activities in which you engage.

References

Knowles, M.S. (1975). *Self-Directed Learning: a guide for learners and teachers.* New York: Associated Press.

Knowles, M.S. (1977). *A history of the adult education movement in the United States: includes adult education institutions through 1976* (Rev. ed.). Huntington, N.Y.: R.E. Krieger Pub. Co.

Noe, R.A. (2009). Learning System Design: A Guide to Creating Effective Learning Initiatives. Alexandria, VA: Society for Human Resource Management (SHRM) Foundation.

Noe, R.A. (2013). Employee Training and Development (6th ed.). Burr Ridge, IL: McGrawHill/Irwin.

WORKSHEET C.1 ADULT LEARNING AND DEVELOPMENT

Instructions: Use this worksheet to identify the different types of development activities in which you've engaged. By showing which activities focused on technical skills versus behavioral skills, you will get a sense of the variety of opportunities that exist for both types of competencies.

Learning Activities Focused on Technical Competencies	Learning Activities Focused on Behavioral Competencies
Example: *Attended a SHRM seminar on talent acquisition: behavioral interviewing*	Example: *Attended a half-day workshop on Critical Evaluation for developing and using HR metrics*
1.	1.
2.	2.
3.	3.
4.	4.
5.	5.
6.	6.
7.	7.
8.	8.
9.	9.
10.	10.

Instructions: This worksheet can be used as a pre-assessment and/or as a post-assessment exercise. Consider the learning activities that you have done to develop your both your technical and behavioral HR competencies, and capture ones that you think were particularly effective—note those that you think were ineffective so that they can be avoided in the future or so that you can modify your approach to these activities. Do the same for activities that were intentionally or unintentionally focused on your behavioral competencies. Be creative in thinking about how you can develop your behavioral competencies—in ways that you have not previously tried.

EXERCISE C.1 DEVELOPMENT EXERCISE: LEARNING PREFERENCES

Instructions: Answer the following questions as a way to prepare for building an effective development plan.

1. Identify and describe two to three of your favorite learning activities. Why are they your favorites? Be specific and identify the events.
 Notes:

_____

_____

2. Identify and describe two to three of your least favorite learning activities. Why are they your least favorite? Be specific and identify the events and what you disliked the most.
Notes:

_____

_____

3. What is your typical approach to learning?
Notes:

_____

_____

4. How has your approach to learning changed over time, and why do you think these changes have occurred?
Notes:

_____

_____

5. When and how do you think you learn the most?
Notes:

_____

_____

6. What are some of your personal challenges in terms of learning?
Notes:

_____

_____

7. What motivates you to learn?
Notes:

_____

_____

8. From what experiences have you learned the most?
 Notes:

_____

_____

Sample Worksheets and Exercises

Appendix D: Sample Worksheets and Exercises

- Worksheet D.1. Inventory of Assessments (Sample)

- Exercise D.1. Questions to Ask Yourself about Business Acumen (Sample)

- Worksheet D.2. Competency Assessment Worksheet (Sample)

- Worksheet D.3. Preparation for Setting Your Competency Development Goals (Sample)

- Worksheet D.4. Observation Plan (Sample)

- Worksheet D.5. Observation Data Collection (Sample)

- Worksheet D.6. Setting Your Competency Goals (Sample)

WORKSHEET D.1 INVENTORY OF ASSESSMENTS (SAMPLE)

Behavioral Competency	Evidence of Performance	At What Level			
		Entry	Mid	Senior	Exec
Business Acumen	Graduate degree		Mid		
Communication	Hogan Assessment		Mid		
	Myers-Briggs Type Indicator (MBTI)		Mid		
Consultation	Course in graduate school	Entry			
	Supervisor feedback		Mid		
Critical Evaluation	SHRM workshop		Mid		
	Supervisor feedback		Mid		
Ethical Practice	Supervisor feedback		Mid		
Global and Cultural Effectiveness	None		None		
Leadership and Navigation	Course in graduate school	Entry			
	SHRM seminar		Mid		
Relationship Management	MBTI		Mid		
	Supervisor feedback		Mid		

Instructions: Read and familiarize yourself with the definitions and descriptions of the eight HR competencies presented in Chapter 2. Additional data can be found on the SHRM website (www.shrm.org/hrcompetencies) or from other sources. Think about where you might find assessment data as identified in Exercise 2.1. Create a more specific inventory, with breakdown, for this worksheet.

Note: You may want to use a fresh sheet for each competency—particularly if you've been in the profession for a while and have had more opportunity for assessment.

EXERCISE D.1 QUESTIONS TO ASK YOURSELF ABOUT BUSINESS ACUMEN—SAMPLE

Instructions: Answer the following questions as part of your self-assessment process.

How important is Business Acumen in your current role?

Business Acumen is important in that I need to understand the financial services industry. At my current level (midcareer), I need to be able to effectively communicate with other managers in other departments about the work they face each day.

How important is Business Acumen to the role to which you immediately aspire, and what will be some of the Business Acumen gaps that you may need to address?

To be promoted to the senior director role, I will need to be able to demonstrate a knowledge of our competition in the financial services industry and to articulate the challenges this industry faces with respect to the economy and evolving technological applications.

EXERCISE D.1 QUESTIONS TO ASK YOURSELF ABOUT BUSINESS ACUMEN— SAMPLE

How important is Business Acumen to the role to which you ultimately aspire?
To be the CHRO for my organization (or any organization), I will need to be able to provide advice on the issues above—not just understand them.

Do other HR professionals in your peer group demonstrate the same Business Acumen?
Some do, and some do not. Those who seem more comfortable and accepted in the organization seem to be able to relate to many operational units with their ability to comfortably discuss relevant metrics and key measurement issues within financial services.

How well do I understand the Business Acumen competency and the proficiency standards?
Pretty well, and I understand financial services, but I don't have a strong understanding of other industries such as health care or those that might influence what happens in financial services. I also need to know more about the major employers in my geographic region, as not knowing may limit me as well.

How well do most HR professionals understand Business Acumen?
I don't know! This is something I need to find out and understand.

How well do you think non-HR professionals in your organization understand the Business Acumen competency for HR professionals?
Most of the managers see me as "HR" and do not always value that I need/want to understand their business. For the ones who do understand, I think I've been able to demonstrate my depth a bit more through specific interactions. When I work with new hiring managers, they seem surprised at how much of the terminology I know and can apply.

Are you concerned that others in your organization will evaluate this competency differently from other competencies? Is this a problem, and if so, why?
Yes. Being seen as "HR" sometimes means that managers don't provide details that will help me to build this competency and even do my job.

In your current role, will you have an opportunity to develop the stated proficiencies for Business Acumen? If not, how have you attempted to develop these proficiencies, and to what degree have you been successful?
To some degree, yes, but I will need to be more active. I think I also need to be more vocal in my desire to develop, not just in HR, but to learn more of the nuances of the business. I should ask Jean how she's done this; she seems quite successful—I'm a 2-3, but she's a 3-4, I think.

Optional Variation: Develop a rating scale to use for each competency so that you are consistent in your own evaluation. For example, you may use a 5-point scale on your performance where 5 is "demonstrates very well," 4 is "demonstrates," 3 is "unsure," 2 is "demonstrates very little," and 1 is "does not demonstrate."

WORKSHEET D.2 COMPETENCY ASSESSMENT WORKSHEET (SAMPLE)

Competency	Importance of this competency to your current role		I am behaviorally competent at which level	Competency compared with colleagues at my level	Opportunity for development	Priority level for addressing development
	NOW High Medium Low	**FUTURE** High Medium Low	Entry Mid Senior Exec	High Medium Low	High Medium Low	High Medium Low
Business Acumen	Med	High	Mid	Med	Med	High
Communication	High	High	Senior	Med	Med	Med
Consultation	Med	High	Mid	Med	Med	Med-High
Critical Evaluation	Med	High	Mid	Med	High	High
Ethical Practice	High	High	Senior	High	Med	Low
Global and Cultural Effectiveness	Low	Med	Exec	Low	Med	Low
Leadership and Navigation	Med	High	Mid	Med	High	Med
Relationship Management	High	High	Senior	High	Med	Med

Comments: Developing business acumen will allow me to be more nimble and to advance more easily; for consultation, I need to learn specific skills and should develop a plan; for critical evaluation I need to develop more analytical skills—both in a formal sense (class) and informally; for ethical practice, I already operate at this level and have been told so by numerous people.

Instructions: Now that you know more about how to define and describe each competency and have identified the existing assessments you have completed and which are available for this analysis, it is time to take the assessment one step further and think about your proficiency, any gaps you might have, and how you want to prioritize addressing your needs.

Note: Only make 2-3 behavioral competencies a high priority for development at one time—more would be unrealistic. Priorities can change.

WORKSHEET D.3 PREPARATION FOR SETTING YOUR COMPETENCY DEVELOPMENT GOALS (SAMPLE)

Competency Vision Statement: To develop my HR behavioral competencies (and technical HR competency) to the point at which I will be successful in obtaining my SHRM-SCP certification. Or to develop my HR behavioral competencies so that I can move to a larger organization and/ or obtain a more senior HR role than I currently hold.

Competency	Development Goal	Development Actions	Timeframe	Status
Business Acumen	Learn more about the financial services industry	Set up networking meetings with technical managers; attend a professional meeting	Within the next 1-3 months	
Communication	Make a professional presentation to others in the org	Observe presentations of others first; identify an opportunity; role-play; conduct presentation	Within 3-6 months	
Consultation	Identify an internal project to provide HR guidance and input	Engage in purposeful discussion with others across the organization to identify an opportunity	Over the course of 6-9 months	
Critical Evaluation				
Ethical Practice				
Global and Cultural Effectiveness				
Leadership and Navigation				
Relationship Management				

Instructions: Create development goals for each competency. Your development actions should include activities that are reflective of the self-directed learning activities highlighted in the book. There may be overlap in your activities in that one activity may help develop multiple competencies. Including a timeline is important to provide a structure and measurability to your efforts. Finally, periodically assessing the status of your goal accomplishment will help keep you on track.

WORKSHEET D.4 OBSERVATION PLAN (SAMPLE)	
Date: February 10, 2017	**Event:** Weekly Staff Meeting
Behavior	Delegation of tasks
Target	Chief HR Officer Sally Smith
Recipient(s) reactions	Direct reports to the CHRO • Generally accepting; some confusion
Outcomes	• How many times was something delegated and to whom? • What technique did the CHRO use, and did the technique vary based on the recipient? • How did the recipients react—both verbally and nonverbally? • Were there outcomes of note that occurred after the meeting
Your reaction	• Did the delegation seem appropriate, and did it feel effective or not?
Target adjustment	Did the CHRO modify the delegation based on reactions? Did it appear that further delegation was used or avoided on the basis of recipient reaction in the room?
Motivation	• Aspire to be running the weekly staff meeting or other similar meetings • If promotion is not imminent due to a lack of movement within, plan to look for a new position within 6-12 months

WORKSHEET D.5 OBSERVATION DATA COLLECTION (SAMPLE)

Target of Observation: Joanne Smith, CHRO, my organization

Observation Scenario: Quarterly strategic update meeting—half-day meeting spanning all organization departments and including all department heads. Smith was the facilitator.

Behaviors noted:	Comments:
• Welcomed and thanked participants	• Set a positive tone
• Explained agenda, noting that time was tight	• Did not ask for input about agenda
• Called on key stakeholders	• Did not state what outcome to be derived
• Highlighted areas of challenge and lack of goal attainment	• Effectively drew in others
• Consistently brought discussion back to a focus on employees	• Effectively communicated problem areas; did not highlight success
• Encouraged and facilitated discussion of problem resolutions	• Maintained a focus on Human Capital with respect to goal attainment
	• Effectively brokered necessary, yet difficult, discussions
	• Effective meeting—but could it have been better if Smith had asked for input on the approach or expected outcomes?
	• Ask Smith if she had an intentional order for the agenda

Overall Observations and Key Takeaways:

Smith was highly influential and effective in getting important issues on the table; key phrase that seemed to help: "I agree with your point, but can you ... ; Smith used silence very effectively, and I need to try this; something I would do differently—I would have asked for more input upfront.

WORKSHEET D.6 SETTING YOUR COMPETENCY GOALS (SAMPLE)				
Critical Evaluation Vision Statement		To be an accomplished and effective critical evaluator in the eyes of my HR leaders and HR colleagues. In the short term, become an expert in measures and metrics so that I can ultimately be able to apply this knowledge to all HR areas across the organization.		
Development Goal	**Development Actions**	**Timeframe**	**Resources Needed**	**Status**
• Learn all existing metrics used for staffing and compensation at my organization • Be able to replicate and explain all of these metrics • Be able to suggest new or additional metrics that will be useful—perhaps even those that are beyond compensation and recruiting	• Set a meeting with our comp specialist to discuss what I need to know/do • Set a meeting with our senior recruiter • Establish a list of specific questions for purposeful discussion that relate to HR measures and metrics • Take a course in HR measures and metrics—supplemented by purposeful discussion with comp and recruiting specialists • Volunteer at a local professional organization (such as a SHRM chapter) to perform an analysis of the membership composition or the budget or both • Look for or develop case vignettes on measures and metrics—specific to my industry first and broader later • Create a journal that relates specifically to measures and metrics where observations and additional development opportunities can be identified	• Within 3 months to meet with colleagues • Within 3 months build discussion plan • Within 12 months take course and build subsequent observation plan • Within 6 months identify cases and begin analyzing • Immediately start the journal	• Time • Cooperation • Budget for professional development • Focus • Case studies specific to metrics • Colleague willing/able to role-play on measurement issues • Notebook or journal on electronic device to capture observations and developmental information	

Endnotes

Introduction

1. Hall, Douglas T. *Careers In and Out of Organizations*. Thousand Oaks, CA: Sage, 2001.

Chapter 1

1. Society for Human Resource Management. Content Validation Study of the SHRM Competency Model. www.shrm.org/HRCompetencies/ PublishingImages/14-0705%20Content%20Validation%20Study%203. pdf and www.shrm.org/LearningAndCareer/competency-model/ Documents/15-0412%20Criterion%20Validation%20Study_FINAL.pdf
2. The SHRM Competency Model can be found at www.shrm.org/ hrcompetencies.
3. Ulrich, David, Wayne Brockbank, Jon Younger, and Mike Ulrich. *Global HR Competencies: Mastering Competitive Value from the Outside-In*. New York: McGraw-Hill, 2012.
4. See www.shrm.org/certification and www.shrm.org/certification/learning.

Chapter 2

1. Myers-Briggs Type Indicator: https://www.cpp.com/products/mbti/index. aspx.

2. DiSC profile assessment: https://www.discprofile.com/what-is-disc/overview/.

Chapter 3

1. All of the competencies are important. However, they may not be equally important at the same time. Importance may vary depending on the level of the individual and the nature of the job or organization.

Chapter 6

1. Barbazette, Jean. *Instant Case Studies: How to Design, Adapt, and Use Case Studies in Training.* San Francisco: Pfeiffer, 2004.
2. This case was contributed by Joe Coombs, senior analyst, Workforce Trends, Society for Human Resource Management.
3. Ibid.

Chapter 7

1. See http://www.quotationspage.com/quotes/Voltaire.
2. See http://www.brainyquote.com/quotes/authors/b/bruce_lee.html.
3. See https://en.wikipedia.org/wiki/Question.
4. Knapp, M., J. Hall, and T. Horgan. Nonverbal Communication in Human Interaction, 8th ed. Boston: Wadsworth Cengage, 2014.

Chapter 8

1. Rosenthal, T., and B. Zimmerman. *Social Learning and Cognition.* New York: Academic Press, 1978.
2. Saul McLeod, "Bandura—Social Learning Theory," Simply Psychology, 2016, http://www.simplypsychology.org/bandura.html.

Chapter 9

1. Rodell, J. B. "Finding Meaning through Volunteering: Why Do Employees Volunteer and What Does It Mean for Their Jobs?" Academy of Management Journal 56, no. 5 (2013): 1274-1294.

2. Geisler, C., M. Okum, and C. Grano. (2014). "Who Is Motivated to Volunteer? A Latent Profile Analysis Linking Volunteer Motivation to Frequency of Volunteering." Psychological Test and Assessment Modeling 56, no. 1 (2014): 3-24.

3. Rodell, J. B. "Finding Meaning through Volunteering."

Chapter 11

1. Tips on how to create an effective business book club can be found in the following sources: www.fastcompany.com/bookclub/group.html; http://www.wikihow.com/Start-a-Business-Book-Club; and Goldfield, Burton M. "Employee Development through Reading—Start a Book Club." Forbes. April 19, 2011. http://www.forbes.com/sites/burtongoldfield/2011/04/19/employee-development-through-reading-start-a-book-club.

Appendix A

1. This case was contributed by Montrese Hamilton, MSLS, librarian, Society for Human Resource Management.

Appendix B

1. Society for Human Resource Management. Content Validation Study of the SHRM Competency Model. www.shrm.org/HRCompetencies/PublishingImages/14-0705%20Content%20Validation%20Study%203.pdf and www.shrm.org/LearningAndCareer/competency-model/Documents/15-0412%20Criterion%20Validation%20Study_FINAL.pdf

2. Please note that all competency models or bodies of knowledge related to any profession will be updated and revalidated on a regular basis—about every five years—give or take a year depending on what is occurring in the profession. While definitions may be modified or proficiencies added or subtracted, the foundational model will usually remain relatively intact.

Index

*Page numbers appended with ill refer to tables,
figures, worksheets, or exercises.*

About the Author

Deb Cohen, Ph.D., is an association executive with more than 25 years of experience advising, speaking, and guiding nonprofit, academic, and for-profit entities. With the publication of this book, Cohen is delivering talks and professional development highlighting how behavior matters to HR professionals and how to develop HR behavioral competencies. As a former senior vice president with the Society for Human Resource Management (SHRM), Cohen was responsible for a 50-person division covering knowledge services, original research, and the development of a professionwide competency model.

A subject matter expert in HR, management, and organizational behavior, Cohen has expertise in creating and executing new initiatives that support and develop organization strategy. Under her direction, research services were transformed into a million-dollar revenue stream, a curriculum guide for the HR profession was established, and a competency model that forms the basis for a worldwide certification credential was created. She received her Ph.D. in management and human resources and her master's degree in labor and human resources from The Ohio State University. She is a certified HR professional with the designation SHRM-SCP.

She is co-author of *Defining HR Success: 9 Critical Competencies for HR Professionals* (2015) and a co-editor of *Developing and Enhancing Teamwork in Organizations: Evidence-Based Best Practices and Guidelines* (2013). Prior to joining SHRM, Cohen spent 15 years as an academician teaching HRM at George Washington and George Mason universities. She has published over 50 articles and book chapters and has been published in such journals as *Academy of Management Journal, Personnel Psychology, Journal of Management, and the Journal of Business Ethics.*

Additional
SHRM-Published Books

101 Sample Write-Ups for Documenting Employee Performance Problems: A Guide to Progressive Discipline & Termination, Second Edition
Paul Falcone

Defining HR Success: 9 Critical Competencies for HR Professionals
Kari R. Strobel, James N. Kurtessis, Debra J. Cohen, and Alexander Alonso

Destination Innovation: HR's Role in Charting the Course
Patricia M. Buhler

The EQ Interview: Finding Employees with High Emotional Intelligence
Adele B. Lynn

The Manager's Guide to HR: Hiring, Firing, Performance Evaluations, Documentation, Benefits, and Everything Else You Need to Know,
Second Edition
Max Muller

The Power of Stay Interviews for Engagement and Retention
Richard P. Finnegan

Stop Bullying at Work: Strategies and Tools for HR, Legal, & Risk ManagementProfessionals, 2nd Edition
Teresa A. Daniel and Gary S. Metcalf

Up, Down, and Sideways: High-Impact Verbal Communication for HR Professionals
Patricia M. Buhler and Joel D. Worden